BLESSED
STRUGGLES

REGINA WILLIAMS

BE MOTIVATED AND INSPIRED BY

BLESSED STRUGGLES

MY JOURNEY FROM EXTREME POVERTY IN KENYA TO
PROFESSIONAL AND POLITICAL SUCCESS IN GREAT BRITAIN

ABOUT THE AUTHOR

Regina Williams' story starts in the rural Kenyan village of Nyankongo, in the town of Kisii, where she faced extreme poverty, and continues through the sand dunes of North Africa, all the way to London. Growing up as one of nine children, Regina learned early on about hard work and resilience. These lessons paid off when she became a skilled project management practitioner, a job that took her across Europe, working on big projects in countries like the UK, Germany, Sweden, and the Netherlands. Her expertise helped improve banks, government departments, and even London's public transport system.

But Regina's heart also led her to public service. For ten years, she served as a councillor in the London Borough of Newham, where she was a voice for the people, tackling their problems and finding solutions. It was a role that filled her with pride, connecting her back to her roots and the community leadership she admired in her mother.

She loves hiking in country parks or walking along the banks of the Thames taking in the London views and sunset, relishing street food, and listening to buskers' music.

Regina's life story, from grinding poverty to becoming a highly recognized project management professional and community leader as well as a real estate portfolio manager in London, is truly both inspiring and motivating - reaffirming that where you begin is not where you will end.

DEDICATION

To my wonderful children, Emmanuel and Jennifer, and our entire family,

This book is dedicated to you with all my love and gratitude. It's because of you, my dear children, that I've worked so hard, making sure you never have to face the challenges I did. Whenever I felt like giving up, thinking of you both gave me the strength to keep going. Being your parent, I feel it's my duty to push through, a task I believe is given to us by God.

Everything I do, from my morning workout to a swim in the pool, is because I want to be there for you two. I dream of being part of your happiest moments and watching you grow into your incredible selves.

I'm also incredibly thankful to God for letting me write and share my story. From arriving in this country alone, pregnant with Emmanuel, and now surrounded by a family full of love, I am humbled by the grace that has guided my path. I feel blessed to call Great Britain my home and for allowing me to build a family here.

To my beloved parents watching over us from heaven, I owe you everything. You raised me with love and wisdom, and I will always hold dear every lesson and blessing you've given me. May your souls rest in eternal peace.

With all my heart,
Your Regina

AYOMA-ARUMBA
L O N D O N

TABLE OF CONTENTS

About the Author 5

Acknowledgements 13

CIRCUMCISION: A RITE OF PASSAGE 15

   The Guardian's Assignment for the Circumcised 18

   The Second Phase: Esuguta 20

   The Third Phase: 'Chinyangi' 21

   The Fourth Phase: Coming Out of the House 23

   Reflections 24

PART I: INTRODUCTION AND EARLY LIFE 27

Chapter 1. Introduction **29**

   My Parents 33

   My Homeland 40

Chapter 2. The Homestead **45**

   Fearsome Nights 53

   Reflections on prayer at home 56

   Family income 58

   Changaa: a homemade, potent illegal spirit 60

Chapter 3. The River **67**

   Washing at the river 69

   Terror at the river 70

   Fun at the river 73

   The journey home from the river 75

Chapter 4. The Food We Ate **76**

   Food at home and the culture of borrowing (egieseri) 76

   Visiting grandmother 78

Malnutrition and disease 80

Food scarcity 82

Pooling resources in the village economy........................... 83

Chapter 5. Christmas.. 86

Preparations 86

The day itself... 91

A sad Christmas 92

Chapter 6. Primary School 93

Nyambera Primary School 94

Switching schools.. 97

Menstruation 99

Chapter 7. Secondary School Education............................... 101

Nyabururu Girl's Secondary School 102

Visting Day... 104

Sourcing water at secondary school 105

Sick in school.. 106

Snacks... 108

Chapter 8. High School 110

Struggles at Mukumu Girls High School........................... 113

Motivation to Succeed at Mukumu High.......................... 115

Results Day.. 116

Resiting A-level exams at Nyabururu Girls 117

Reflections on secondary education.................................... 118

Chapter 9. Life in a Catholic Church Mission 121

Reflections on life in the mission....................................... 124

Mum, the village elder... 128

My first job 129

PART II: FROM KENYA TO MOROCCO, ... 131
MOROCCO TO ENGLAND

Chapter 10. The Scholarship that Changed My Life 133

Arrival in the capital.. 138

Chapter 11. Life in Morocco.. 144

Chapter 12. Exit Morocco, Enter Great Britain 149

University – different course, different country, same aim . 156

Revisiting The Daily Journey 166

Another Round of Education.. 171

Revisiting Middlesex university after 23 years.................... 175

Chapter 13. Work After Graduation 176

Work in UK and Europe 181

Project Management 187

Chapter 14. For Ten Years an Elected Representative 189

Volunteering in the Community 208

Chapter 15. Discovering My Date of Birth 209

PART III: DEALING WITH GRIEF.................................. 213

Chapter 16. Deaths in the Family 215

Dad's death 4th May 1997 215

Alex's death 1st April 2003... 217

Mum's death 13th September 2021 221

William's death 13th December 2021 228

PART IV: CONCLUSION 233

Chapter 17. My Dreams Were to Come True 238

Chapter 18. Testimonies 251

Testimony from Kate Davies, UK 254

Testimony from Pamela, Kenya... 257

Chapter 19. In Conclusion 260

ACKNOWLEDGEMENTS

I want to express my deepest gratitude to each of you who have contributed to shaping my autobiography. Your dedication and expertise have been instrumental in shaping this book into its best version.

Firstly, a heartfelt thank you to my family for their unwavering support and patience. Your guidance was crucial during challenging moments, and I am grateful for the strength you provided throughout this journey.

I extend my appreciation to my initial editor, Gladys Kwamboka. The open and insightful dialogue stemming from our shared cultural background enriched the editing process.

Special thanks to Kwendo Wellington for your remarkable contributions. Your insights added depth to my autobiography, and I'm thankful for the unique perspective you brought to the project.

To Chris Oswald, I am truly grateful for your meticulous review, which significantly contributed to establishing the structure and flow of the book.

Lastly, a sincere thank you to my final editor, Sanjana Verma. Entrusted with the crucial task of proofreading and final polish editing, your invaluable contribution in the final phase is deeply appreciated.

Each of you has played a vital role, and I extend my sincere gratitude for the great work and dedication you invested in my autobiography. Thank you all.

CIRCUMCISION:
A RITE OF PASSAGE

Female circumcision was an age-old practice in my community in Kisii, Kenya. The Abagusii people had engaged in it for centuries. Although my mum was born in the 1920s and grew up in a society where this was the norm, she didn't support this practice. In fact, she had resolved that my little sister Stella and I would not undergo this ritual.

Unfortunately, despite my mother's disapproval, when I reached the age for circumcision according to our tribal customs, my older sister, Philomena, hid me from her to make sure it happened. She took me at bedtime, joining other girls waiting for the knife. We laughed and joked, but I was sick with fear inside. I had no choice but to follow tradition, knowing it would cause intense discomfort. After all, it was a tradition. It was how it had always been done. There was a belief that no man would marry an uncircumcised woman, leading to potential rejection within the community.

In the early morning, my sister delivered me to the circumcision performers. They were elderly women equipped with razor blades.

Circumcision marked a passage to womanhood in our community. Ten of us who were going to be circumcised, all aged about seven to nine years old, were assembled under a banana tree. We looked frightened because we were, even though we were deemed grown enough for womanhood.

There was honour in being put forward, mixed with intense fear of the hurt to come. Still, I wanted to go ahead with it. I didn't want to be an outcast in the community.

When it was my turn, I struggled, I fought, and I screamed. The terror of that burning, piercing pain stays with me even today, half a century later. There was no anaesthesia, just the knife. When we bled, they patched us up with a paste made from millet flour. The blade pierced the skin, cutting deep into us, and then we waited for the rest of the girls to be done.

Yet, like the others, I had to do it. The pain enveloped me. Then, all I wanted was for it to stop. Nothing else. I just wanted it to stop. I cried and even attempted to run away, half cut, with blood running down my legs, wishing that my mum was there to rescue me. But she was not there, nor was my sister. I remember running away and standing far from the woman who was cutting me, crying, my hands folded around my chest, cold and shivering, until they begged me to come back, to sit down, and have the procedure finished. They were telling me, 'We must finish. Where will you go with your skin cut and hanging?' I finally agreed to go back and sit on the stone. Two or three women held my legs apart, and another held my chest back so that I couldn't move until the cutting was finished.

The others around me were happy: dancing, rejoicing for those who had endured circumcision without crying, and celebrating. Meanwhile, I was full of pain, all done without my mother's knowledge or her comforting presence.

Worse than the pain, however, was the reaction from others because I fought and resisted the knife. I struggled and refused to stay still. There was no sympathy for me at all. Instead, I was bullied, ostracised even, because I went against tradition, against the accepted way since time began. My screams were seen as cowardice, and I was frequently reminded of this in the years ahead. My family did not know what I was going through psychologically, and I had no support. I was in my own world, tormented by bullies because of my crying, which was a natural response to the pain I had to endure. It's no exaggeration to say that my resistance to this cruelty and my fear of the blade marked my childhood and set me apart.

Bullied and tormented in the village, I was the girl who could not go through her transition to womanhood courageously, proudly, and in dignified silence. Crying during circumcision was a big taboo, according to the Kisii tradition. I was accused of bringing shame not only to myself but also to my family, my clan, and the entire village. I was labelled 'enkuri', meaning 'cry'. My crying, so the story spread in the community, would perhaps have been mitigated had I remained still throughout the ritual. But I had made an unpleasant situation worse by standing up and attempting to run away halfway through the process with my blood running down my legs. I was a child on a cold, early morning, wearing no clothes but a small, scarf-like material around my shoulders. I was freezing, but one could only be covered after a successful circumcision. As I had shown fear, any cover for me would depend on the mercy and discretion of the women conducting the ceremony. I just stood there, ignored, alone, shivering, crying, and still missing my Mum,

The women who performed the circumcision lacked formal education and understanding of the potential consequences of circumcision on the female reproductive system. They used their bare hands to navigate the layers they wanted to cut.

Each girl was brought to her own home to start a three to four-week seclusion period. My Mum was shocked when she found out that I was among those who had been circumcised, something she had not planned for. Hearing about the pain I went through deeply troubled her. She sought to comfort me while expressing her disappointment in Philomena for keeping this from her. But the people told her to cool down —'maziwa yakimwagika hayachoteki,' meaning 'spilled milk cannot be scooped back.'

The Guardian's Assignment for the Circumcised

From this time on, each girl is assigned a guardian ('Omosegi'). This individual takes care of the circumcised girl within the household. They are allowed to enter the secluded area where the circumcised girl stays and provide continuous support until the completion of her seclusion period. This role entails significant responsibility as it fosters a lasting relationship between the guardian and the girl, extending beyond the seclusion period into their lives.

The newly initiated young girls were greeted with a celebration in their homes. In my case, there was no feasting or celebration because my mother was unaware that I had gone for circumcision. Therefore, there were no arrangements for food or drinks at my home. I was the last girl to be accompanied home due to my crying during the circumcision.

There was no going out of the house for newly circumcised girls, and no visitors were allowed to see us. If a visitor came to the door, the circumcised girl was first alerted to hide before the visitor was welcomed inside. During this period, the girl's body would be smeared with ash except for the eyes, nostrils, hair, and mouth. People were not supposed to recognise us if we ventured outside the house. This ash would only be washed away on the day our seclusion ended, which we called the coming out day.

On that day, there was singing, dancing, and ululating (okoiririata). The girls were welcomed into the community as mature women, even though none of us had reached puberty yet.

The Second Phase: Esuguta

The Esuguta ceremony was the next event, taking place two weeks after circumcision. It involved the planting of a special grass called Esuguta, traditionally used to make brooms. This ceremony typically took place in the evening. A group of girls escorted me to gather and uproot the Esuguta grass, bring it home, and plant it in the corner of the room where I stayed. The day concluded with a family gathering, where fermented porridge sweetened with sugar was served, a rare treat.

Once the Esuguta was planted, it became an integral part of my daily routine. Regularly watering it served as a practical task and a symbol of my care for the plant, signifying my transition to adulthood.

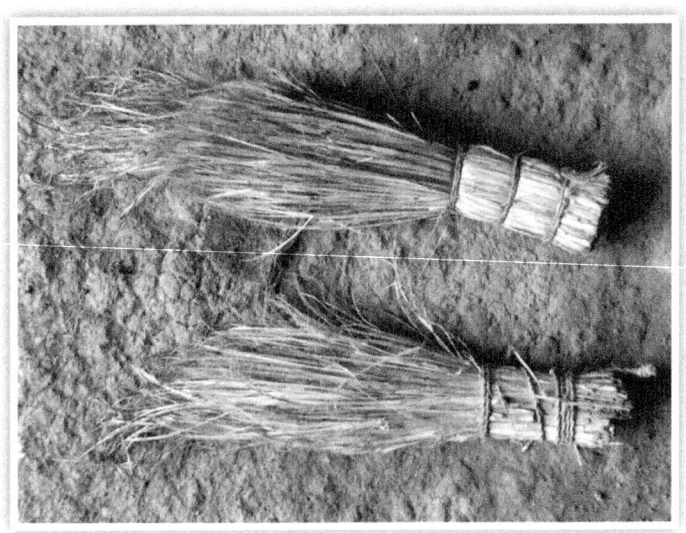

The Esugata plant

The Third Phase: 'Chinyangi'

In this ceremony, known as 'Chinyangi' (weddings) in the Kisii dialect, elder women and older girls gathered at our family's home in the evening, four weeks after circumcision. I was secluded in one room while they were in the next. They told me that in that adjacent room, a giant snake (Echage) had been brought in specifically to offer punishment for my past wrongdoings and finally take me away. This filled me with intense fear.

> They were singing in Kisii as follows:
> *'Kame Echage oyaye, Kame the Echage*
> *oyaye, Kame Echage nomware yachakuoyia'*
> (Milk the snake, milk the snake because it has come to take the circumcised girl)

These words were repeated rhythmically, mimicking the sound of a snake rolling. All individuals in the room participated in singing this song, creating a musical atmosphere as if the snake was joyous or pleased.

The snake was believed to have the power to punish, forgive, or swallow me whole. The idea of being swallowed scared me the most. At that young age, I genuinely believed this would happen in the next room. Questions were directed at the snake, and its responses were either 'yes, yes,' or 'no, no.' They even asked the snake if they could offer it all the good things in the world in exchange for sparing me, to which the snake replied, 'No, no.'

My screams filled the room as I grappled with intense fear. On this day, people came to report any wrongdoings I had committed against them over the years. For example, they mentioned times I refused to give them a cup of water when I met them coming from the river, and they were thirsty. The idea was that the snake would punish me. It felt like judgment day, and I was overwhelmed by fear, desperately pleading for forgiveness and making vows to become a better person.

Even when they were bringing me to the next room to reveal the truth while saying there was no snake, I couldn't shake my belief in the snake's existence. I was dragged along, convinced that the snake was real. But to my surprise, when they finally brought me into the adjacent room, they assured me there was no actual snake. It was, in fact, a musical instrument made from two special bamboo sticks that were rubbed together against a wet cow skin placed on top of an African clay pot. The pot featured a fastening around its neck, designed to produce musical sounds when sticks were rubbed against it. This contraption created the sounds I had believed were coming from the snake. The instrument was specifically designed to mimic a snake's voice, producing the distinctive 'yes, yes' and 'no, no' sounds that filled me with terror.

After that, I was warned to never tell the uncircumcised girls about this, as it would bring bad omens to my life. I never even told my sister, Stella, when her time came. I believed they had good intentions for us.

The Fourth Phase: Coming Out of the House

In the fourth phase, referred to as 'coming out of the house,' we marked the end of seclusion. This occurred two days after the unsettling 'Chinyangi' event, and it signified the first time I had been in public in roughly four weeks since my circumcision. It was a festive occasion where people were invited home to eat large meals and indulge in drinks. However, my heart held no joy because I knew that news of my tears during the circumcision had spread, and I expected to face bullies.

The final ceremony included a thorough bath because, during the four-week period of seclusion after my circumcision, my body had been covered in ash. Therefore, on the last day of seclusion, I had a thorough bath, with a guardian assisting me in the process. This involved dressing me in new clothes, applying cow fat or Vaseline to my body, grooming my eyebrows, and presenting myself to the public for the first time since the circumcision. During seclusion, the circumcised don't put on clothes.

The transition was celebrated with new outfits, gifts, and festivities. I received a stern warning again to never reveal the secrets of our cultural traditions, especially the part about the snake, to other young, uncircumcised girls, as it held significant importance within our culture.

Then, finally, the elderly woman came with fresh milk in her mouth and sprayed it on my face. Dad gulped alcohol called 'busa' in his mouth, and sprayed it on my face, all done as a sign of blessing me into the world.

Reflections

Millions of Kenyan women have undergone similar rituals to the ones I experienced as a young girl, pushed on by this driving force called tradition. This tradition cut into our flesh like an army invading a defenseless land, plundering through skin and tissue.

It was finally, and thankfully, banned by the Kenyan government with the passing of the Prohibition of Female Genital Mutilation Act on 30th September 2011. My mother never wanted it for any of us, and later, after the prohibition, she worked with the tribal chief to discourage the practice. That didn't save me from the pain at the time.

The law of 2011 has helped reduce it, but it still happens today. It's tough to change tradition—to change the way it has always been done. During Covid, female genital mutilation increased. There remains a long road to eradicating FGM in the world we live in. This terrible practice causes both physical and psychological problems for the victims throughout their lifetime.

We believed our very future depended on the circumcision, as they told us. We would never get suitors, much less offers of marriage, if we did not get circumcised.

But now, some men in the country are saying they will only marry girls who are not circumcised to support the ban on this cruel and inhumane practice.

A rite of passage suggests a journey from one state of mind or maturity to another. My life has been a journey, but circumcision made no part of that. Yes, we were now considered women rather than girls, but as you turn the pages of this autobiography, you will see that our maturity was forced upon us by necessity, not by the knife. My childhood was stunted, short, and full of horror; yet without that horror and taboo, or the extreme poverty and hunger, would I have found the strength and resilience to embark upon such an extraordinary journey? Everything from the earliest days of my life built up inside me, bringing with it the determination to make a change. And that necessitated a long and difficult journey, both in terms of miles travelled and barriers to overcome.

We are who we are because of the meeting of two things: our experiences, particularly in our early lives, and the attitude we have toward those experiences. The two combine to produce the driving force in our lives, as well as the essence of who we are.

I realised afterwards that, however punishing a situation is, there's always someone who has it worse than me. And the only way I could turn things around was with a good education. Thus, my education, not the horrors of circumcision, became my true rite of passage to a wider, better world. And that, as you shall see, was fraught with hardship.

PART I:

INTRODUCTION
AND EARLY LIFE

CHAPTER ONE
INTRODUCTION

I was born into poverty in the hills of Kisii, Kenya. My first expedition was to the bustling capital, Nairobi, and then traversing across Africa to Morocco to study medicine in an unfamiliar language in Casablanca. My path took an unexpected turn, leading to a detour to the UK during the Gulf War.

Young, naive, pregnant, and with only $50, I landed in Britain, where I knew nobody. Now I am a successful investor with a masters degree in IT, and a project management practitioner who has worked on major projects across Europe. Apart from this, I served as the first black female East African Politician in London during ten years as an elected representative of the people.

I hope to inspire others with my faith, self-belief, determination, courage, and resilience as I outline the highs and lows of this lifelong journey. My life, as you will see in this autobiography, is a testament to the resilience epitomized by the Swahili mantra 'maisha ni kupambana'—life is a struggle.

Within these pages, you will see the hardships I faced in life and the challenges that threatened to pull me down. Yet, you'll also witness the spirit that carried me through. How I overcame these challenges is the heart of this autobiography—'songa mbele,' move forward, as we say in Swahili. Just as the wildebeest in the Mara River fights back against the crocodiles and hippos, when crossing the river between Kenya and Tanzania in search of grass, I fought back against hardships, deprivation, hunger, fear, bullying, and taboo to emerge victorious. I was not consumed. I am a fighter.

Join me on this journey of willpower, success, and an unyielding spirit that refuses to surrender. As I share the mantra 'Never give up,' I invite you to draw strength from my story and believe that you, too, can overcome the challenges in your own journey. Through these pages, you'll discover that the struggles we face in life are stepping stones to our success. So, when I tell you, 'Never give up,' you will find the inspiration to carry on and thrive.

My name is Regina Williams. I was born in Kisii, Kenya, as the sixth child of my parents. I have been residing in the UK for the past 33 years.

This autobiography marks my first literary venture. I have drawn inspiration from the immense hardships I have experienced in my journey, especially during my challenging childhood in Kenya and as a foreigner in Morocco and Great Britain. These experiences have motivated me to share my story and inspire others. Despite encountering numerous obstacles and navigating through peaks and valleys, I have never surrendered. I believe in showcasing the possibility of resilience and perseverance; I will encourage you to persist until you emerge victorious, just as I did.

My journey took many turns, as you shall see in the pages of this book, and it still continues. I want you to read my life story and feel reinvigorated and motivated to renew the fight to make something of your life. I hope my book will achieve just that. Today, from that humble background, I am a holder of two IT-based degrees, a former elected London Borough councillor (2000-2010) and the first black female East African Politician in London, a qualified project management practitioner with work experience in the UK and several European countries, and a certified Microsoft Technology Specialist.

I'm not here to show off, but I'm incredibly proud to share with you my achievements against all odds and to show you that there is hope if you try. I am a real estate entrepreneur in London, having come from rural Kenya and a house that had holes in the roof, which meant that we saw stars through the roof and were soaked by rain that came through those same holes. I am saying this to inspire, motivate, and show that there is hope, particularly for those who have risen from backgrounds of extreme poverty like me. I am living proof that you should never surrender to your circumstances but keep your gaze firmly fixed on the future and chase your dreams with relentless determination, just as I did.

It has been a long journey from my origins. Often, despair has travelled with me, tempting me to give up. Fear and hunger have been my companions, wearing down my body and spirit.

I felt like all I needed was to see a way forward and I could improve my life. I'm also grateful for the people I've touched, motivated, and assisted along the way. You will see some testimonies of these in the testimony section of the book.

As a medical student in Casablanca, Morocco, I again suffered from hunger, which had tormented me in my childhood and throughout my education in Kenya. My body was emaciated due to lack of food, which hollowed out my face and made my teeth protrude. I was sick with no money to buy medicine. Yet, I somehow persevered despite the hunger, and later in the UK, my body blossomed back, like a lily in the valley.

A foreigner far away from my homeland, faith in God was my anchor. I knew that God would not let me sink with problems. So, during my loneliest moments, I turned to God for solace. Ever since my childhood, I have been accompanied by the unwavering presence of God, helping me to navigate this journey and showing me the way when my eyes cannot see. Even in the UK, it was hard initially, especially in the first three years after my arrival. There were serious challenges: money, food, clothes, almost being homeless, and my pregnancy. But thank God for the Christian people who took me in week after week,

You will see this in the pictures through the pages of this book. I regained my strength and vitality.

My early focus was on education, working hard to get a decent job to support myself and my family. At the time, my older sister, Teresa, was the only one working. However, getting an education in such poverty was a monumental challenge. Lack of school fees, being unable to pay even a small amount for building fund contributions and lacking even basic supplies like uniforms and books often kept me out of school for very long periods. Catching up with missed lessons was stressful, and the lack of basic amenities like toilets, electricity, and running water at home only added to the difficulties. We did not have a proper house and slept with fear. No watch or phones, being woken up by the rooster's crows, or birds singing in the morning—sweet sounds but not for that purpose.

I started making a traditional beer called changaa to raise money for my primary school fees and even to buy exercise books, pencils, uniforms, and food.

Despite these obstacles, I persevered like a cactus tree in the desert, conquering all adversities.

I hope my story motivates you to believe in your own ability to overcome any obstacles and create a better future for yourself and your family. No matter how difficult the journey may seem, the motto 'songa mbele' (step forward) should always be embraced to find the strength to lead you to success.

My Parents

My mother, Magdalene, was a dark-skinned woman of medium build, about five feet three inches tall. She plaited her hair at night before going to bed and undid it in the morning.

My parents in front of the avocado tree at our Ichuni home in 1987.

My mother had no formal education. Nevertheless, she was knowledgeable and knew the value of education. She was also a prayerful, generous, forgiving, loving, kind, and warm person.

My mum was a people person and a good cook. She always dressed well and presented herself neatly and cleanly. I remember her as a caring, generous, trustworthy and open person with no malice towards anyone. She became a community leader, sharing and giving to the vulnerable.

She gave what she had freely. She shared without any thought of saving it for her children. She was selfless. She lived each day as it came, never worrying about tomorrow. She was a strong believer in God and a committed Catholic. 'Let tomorrow take care of itself,' was her motto. She never judged people—she left that to God. And she never took sides, even with her children.

Mum was strong when she was young. She spent her time cooking and talking to neighbours and friends. In her early years, she joined a convent, hoping to become a nun, but was pulled out to get married so that her brothers could get the cows from her dowry to pay for their wives. This was the culture, and she did not refuse, so her dream of being a nun was stopped for her brothers.

Mum was a member of the Catholic women's association in Narok. She had moved from Kisii, our homeland in Western Kenya, where she was also a member of the Catholic women's association in Kisii Parish. The woman who never even knew how to write her name became a community leader in my village of Nyakongo. She acted as the local chief's representative in meetings when he was unavailable. Holding gatherings within the community, she would listen to the concerns of the residents and take the necessary actions to resolve or escalate matters to the chief as required. She signed papers or forms with her fingerprints. Later in life, after a lengthy illness, she moved to Narok in south-western Kenya, west of Nairobi, along the Great Rift Valley, to stay with my sister, Teresa.

My mother holding Cynthia, Teresa's daughter and Lawrence,
Philomena's son, Lawrence, and Cynthia her first grandchildren.
To the right is my little sister Stella, 1970s.

Mum didn't believe in hard work and struggle in life. She lived day by day, trusting in God. It worked for her. Mum gave birth to nine children, of which I was the sixth born, but three died at birth. The firstborn, Alloys Tumbo, and the fifth born, twins David and Ogega, died due to breech presentations. In those days, women gave birth at home, assisted by traditional birth attendants who were not equipped to handle complicated deliveries or any postnatal complications. My surviving siblings are Teresa, Philomena, Ken, and Stella. My fourth sibling, Alex, passed away at the age of forty-five after relocating and settling in the USA. Even to this day, this loss continues to pain me deeply; it was a big blow to our family.

Now, coming to my dad, William Mageto. He was tall, dark, and slim. He was away from home most of the time, so I spent little time with him. He kept his hair long and combed, styled with a side parting that was popular in the 1950s and 60s. He had excellent communication skills and wrote speeches for the local senior chief. He was taught by British colonists in Kenya. According to his friends, his manner of speaking resembled that of an Englishman. They often joked that if he spoke from behind curtains, he would be mistaken for an Englishman. He was a reserved man who measured his words and believed in the power of reasoned argument and persuasion to solve disagreements.

My dad was educated at the Government School, Kisii, the precursor of the prestigious Kisii High School, the alma mater of some of the best brains among the Abagusii and other tribes.

I learned from my dad's peers that he was nicknamed Carey Francis because he was good at mathematics. Francis, an Englishman from Cambridge, was a famous mathematics teacher at Alliance High School in Kenya from 1940-1962. Even though my parents were poor, they were kind-hearted people who genuinely cared for us.

The earliest family snapshot of my dad and my brother Alex

My dad passed away in 1997 at the age of 74 years. He succumbed to undiagnosed chest infections. I did not know my father as closely as I would have liked to; he worked and lived away from the family home for a long time. My mum, Magdalene, died on 13th September 2021. She suffered from Alzheimer's disease and could no longer recognise her children. She would sometimes confuse and forget the names of my brothers and sisters, but somehow, she never forgot me.

I have vivid memories of my dad and mum, alongside their friends, gathering and sharing moments of singing and dancing, often after enjoying a drink. Their ability to create joyous moments even without any musical instruments was amazing; people would often join in and start dancing. I wonder if there will be a singer from my dad's side of the family; that talent is still to come out in our family.

I missed the daughter-father bonding. In fact, I never knew Dad when he was strong, as my older siblings did, because I lived with my mum. I knew him when his health had started to decline, although he remained a nice, charming man with a great passion for gardening.

Dad used to call me Nyangige Baba, his mother's name. I miss him a lot. I desperately miss not telling my dad that I loved him; it was not a cultural norm to do so. I hope he knew that only tradition stopped me from expressing my love for him.

Unlike my dad, Mum was a real presence in my early life. We realised that due to poverty, both of my parents may have been depressed, and with no support systems, they were unable to cope with supporting their family as they would have loved. So, we siblings were left to work out the mess. I do not blame my parents because the deprivation I saw gave me reason to pursue every opportunity that came my way.

My Homeland

The Abagusii, one of the ethnic communities in Kenya, are cultivating people whose land-use involves mixed small-scale farming, with maize and bananas as the main food crops. Some people grow coffee and tea as cash crops. The lower part of Kisii, where I was born, is densely populated.

It is said that before the arrival of the British colonialists, Kisii town (then known as Getembe) was a place with abundant trees where elders held their traditional courts. With the increase in colonial interest in the area, it became heavily populated by the British. The locals nicknamed it Bosongo, which translates as 'place of white people.' After colonialism, it acquired the name Kisii, the town of Kisii people, which is a variation of the name of the local community, Abagusii. The community is also believed to take its name from its patriarch, Omogusii.

My dad, who was working in the town of Nakuru, had taken my brothers with him. We girls had to do the heavy work that the running of the household depended on, like clearing brushes and fetching firewood and water. The absence of men in the household made life much harder. It also left us with less protection from petty criminals, adding a great deal of fear to our everyday routines. Memories of that fear still stay with me today, making me shudder to think about what we endured for survival.

My dad, William, my two brothers—Alex on the left and Ken
on the right, in a place called Paul Machanga in Nakuru, Kenya

My friend, Cecilia Obutu, was one of the few dependable people I had around me in my childhood. We planned our household chores together, prioritising tasks and deciding on our focus. Often, we would start by fetching water, then go searching for peas or kale, tomatoes growing wildly, or any other vegetables, and finally get firewood from the bushes. I would call my friend's name at the top of my voice in Ekegusii. Since we had no phones, I would shout her name loudly, and she would shout back just as loudly. Then, we would decide whether to go to the river, gather firewood, or sweep the compounds, sharing our plans in that shouting. We were well-organised, and this friendship helped us achieve our daily tasks.

With my real childhood friend Obutu (to the right) in about 1979.
The only friend I had from my homeland. My sister Teresa purchased
these clothes for us; we had never had decent clothes before this.

We would carry water in pails on our heads from the river, storing it in larger pots in the house. But if your family, like mine, lacked enough big pots for storage, you went to the river daily and sometimes twice a day. If you had visitors or washing to do, then you would make many more trips to and from the river in a day. Walking to the river was a hefty task, paired with the fear that I would meet young boys at the river who would catapult stones or fruit at me. It made me miserable whenever I had to walk to the river to get water for cooking and washing the utensils. It became an unpleasant chore, as my book will explain. There was also bullying at the river, as I was seen as an outcast coward who cried during circumcision, which was a big taboo.

Going to the river was among the many chores I faced every day. We were either cleaning the compound, looking for food, or cooking. My day started early morning and ended late evening, leaving little time for play or relaxation. There were no game facilities in the village. The few schools near my home had sports fields, but you could only use them during school hours. Many of us lacked access to any form of sports facility, so we resorted to playing hide and seek around our households.

However, children found unoccupied spaces, made them their own, and came up with games that we played according to our own rules. The girls found pieces of cloth and sisal and made skipping ropes, soon skipping away happily, laughing, giggling, and teasing each other. We also played netball and rounders and engaged in hop, skip, jump, and hide and seek. The boys improvised with scraps and pieces of cloth, banana fibres, and string to produce almost round objects, which they called footballs. Football was only for the boys. They used sticks or stones as goalposts and bingo; it was time for a football game. Despite our limited resources, we found joy and creativity in making the most of what we had for our games and playtime. Soon, the day was gone, or mum or dad called, and it was time to end the joyous evening.

Despite coming from a two-parent household, my older siblings and I took on parenting roles as children. There were times when we had to look after our parents, especially when they were drunk. It often fell upon me to ensure their safety and prevent any risk of choking on their vomit. Witnessing them in such a condition was distressing, and I would have to clean up the aftermath the following day. Although it was not a daily occurrence, these incidents, happening about twice a week, were difficult to bear. Alongside this responsibility, I also had to care for my younger siblings when our parents could not.

At times, I draw a parallel between myself and the cactus tree, a resilient symbol that retains its vitality even amidst the harshest droughts. I believe I must share the testimony of hope with others because I know many will benefit from reading my story, and I hope it helps you, whatever your circumstances are.

This is my tale of my *blessed struggles*.

CHAPTER TWO
THE HOMESTEAD

My earliest memories of my childhood in Nyankongo village are filled with experiences of hardship, deprivation, loneliness, and sadness. Living conditions in Nyankongo were harsh. There were no tarmacked roads, piped water or electricity in the homes. There were many unemployed people, both young and old. Many of those young people had dropped out of school due to an inability to pay school fees, which helped swell the groups of idle people. This, inevitably, led to petty crimes, such as stealing ripe bananas, harvesting others' maize, or chasing and catching people's hens to sell to others. Some even resorted to stealing cattle. People would often wake up to find their prized cow gone. The owners would scream, calling village men to follow the tracks and catch the thieves. When you have very little, every loss is critical. My family had less than most, yet we suffered from thieves sneaking into our compound at night.

Most land, ours included, could not produce enough food to feed the families that owned it. We did not have dairy cattle and could not produce enough beans, maize, or vegetables from our inadequate plot for subsistence. We would often go to our grandmother Salome and Aunt Eusebia (pronounced Yosabia) for vegetables and dry maize for ugali flour. My mum occasionally leased land, tilled it, and planted it. That gave us a little more maize and a few more beans. But she could only do so much. Most of the time, she did not manage to lease any land at all.

A house like my childhood home.

When I was a child, we lived in a grass-thatched house. It was very primitive: mud-walled with a round structure, we shared it with our chickens, dog and goat as we couldn't afford a shed or coop. If we tethered the goat somewhere in the compound at night, it would have been stolen. So, the goat had a small pen, called 'Egora', attached to the outside of the house. Our house was meant to have windows; it even had gaps designed for them, but we couldn't afford them, so pieces of rusted iron sheets sealed these spaces. The house didn't even have a proper door. The locks comprised pieces of wood that were poorly fastened, diagonally, and across.

Even now, when I am in my sturdy house in the UK, I still get recurring dreams of being back in that Kisii mud house. I wake up, and for a second, I fear that intruders will barge in because we do not have a secure door, only to realise that I am no longer there.

Our roof had holes. If Mum failed to get repairs done on the roof, we ended up seeing starlight coming through at night. When it rained heavily, chilly winds rushed in, along with the rain, and our bedding got wet. We even had to place containers inside the house to catch the rainwater, preventing it from spreading throughout and making it wet and muddy. We moved around at night in search of a dry spot.

Sometimes, because the ground was not cemented, safari ants attacked at night. If we were lucky to have a piece of tyre, we could burn it and direct the smoke to the cracks where they were coming from to force them to retreat; that night, there would be no sleep, and even if the ants desisted from attempting to eat us, we would have the stench of burning rubber pervading our home. And at night, fear consumed us, and we dared not open the door to let the smoke out.

Sometimes, in our mud house, rats would nibble Mum's dry-skinned heels during her drunken nights. The morning would reveal the damage caused by these rats.

My son pictured in a mud house in Kisii in 1999.
As you can see, the house still lacked windows.

The house above was far more an improvement from my childhood house. With an iron sheet roof, there were no holes, which meant we experienced complete darkness at night, allowing us to sleep undisturbed by starlight. Additionally, if it rained at night, we remained dry indoors. During daytime showers, our primitive gutters, like the one above my son's head in the picture on the next page, efficiently trapped rainwater. This helped us avoid trips to the river after rainfall, as we collected and stored water in our containers. These modifications significantly enhanced the convenience and quality of life in our home. We still experienced safari ants here and rats.

In this picture, you can see that our houses had no doors.

Mum's only formal job was working as a labourer at the local coffee factory. She, amongst other women, sorted the coffee berries, left them to dry, and packed them in gunny sacks ready for dispatch.

At times, Mum would come home with worn-out sisal bags she had been given. She repurposed them, cutting them open and turning them into bedding. We used hides or bamboo mats as our mattresses. We covered ourselves with sacks, and they were warm. We put them on top of a small sheet or old blanket for comfort. This was like a sisal mat, so I guess it was not too bad.

The Mosasa coffee factory in Kisii was once my mother's workplace.

Later, my mum found enormous satisfaction from contributing to village life and emerged as a significant community leader.

In 1976, when I was about 14 years old, my sister Teresa graduated from the University of Nairobi. She bought us mattresses and blankets, beds, our first table, and a kerosene stove (for making meals when there is no firewood or when visitors come, and you want to cook without the smoke from firewood). She gave us our first kerosene lantern, a torch, and a dining table with six chairs to sit on. Before this, we used to sit on sections of tree trunks (called 'Egiteni' in Kisii dialect) that we used as chairs.

Egiteni

She also bought a teapot, cups, and plates. We had nothing before.

Also, I can't remember using toothpaste or toothbrush during my early childhood. To brush our teeth, we used a mswak, a plant that we would chew at the end to make the toothbrush. To whiten my teeth, I would use charcoal. It wasn't until secondary school that I came to know about toothbrushes and toothpaste. We also believed that chewing sugarcane helped to clean and strengthen our teeth.

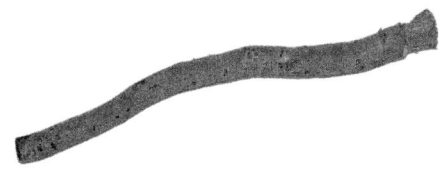

Mswak stick, used as a toothbrush, like the ones I had when I was growing up. This is used without any toothpaste.

51

We used pit latrines and had no tissues. Sometimes, there were no pit latrines available, so we used bushes or fallow land as lavatories. We used all manner of leaves, the best of which were soft, wide ones known as 'emeroka', as we didn't have any tissues. This risked all forms of infections because the leaves could have harboured insect larvae or nettles. In our school, the latrines reserved for teachers had newspapers to use as tissues. I first encountered tissue when I went to secondary school at the age of seventeen. I had never seen tissues before that.

This is the type of lamp I used during my childhood to do my homework.

When it rained and nobody was at home, we would return to our thatched grass-roofed home to find our bedding of hides and sacks drenched. If it started raining when we were at home, we would quickly move our possessions from one place to another to ensure they were not soaked. Eventually, we would find ourselves all huddled together in one corner, cosy but hardly conducive to sleep, or to doing homework, for that matter.

We improvised in many areas of life because we had to. We often used razor blades as nail cutters and sometimes our teeth to trim our long nails. If necessary, I would go to a neighbour to ask if we could use their razor blade. I didn't know what phones looked like or how they were used until I came to England. People who were familiar with phones went to Kisii to make calls from the public telephones at the Post Office. I did not see a computer until I was over twenty-seven years old, after becoming a resident of the UK.

Fearsome Nights

We lived in fear of many dangers in Nyankongo. There were holes in the pieces of iron sheets that sealed off the spaces that were to have been windows. We feared some bad people would be peeping through and watching us. We feared looking towards our windows because we thought we would see them looking at us. It is a fear that I have never lived down. Can you imagine not being comfortable looking towards your own window lest you see somebody trying to get in?

We never used to talk at night, just whispering in case somebody outside heard our location in the house and would break in. We longed for the morning, as it was less likely intruders would enter our flimsy house. Although the days were hot, the nights were cold. We had no blankets to keep ourselves warm at night. We lived one day at a time, getting through the next hurdle, whether it was the cold, fear of attack or bullying, hunger or just the workload on our slender shoulders. We had no choice but to take one hurdle at a time.

We girls missed our dad and brothers. In our rural setting, girls looked up to their brothers and fathers for security. When they were present in the compound with us, we never feared being harassed or bullied. At night, with the men around, we slept soundly in the knowledge that we had protection. However, this reassurance was rare because Dad and my brothers were often away during my early life. Dad was hardly ever at home. My older brother, Alex, went abroad. Soon afterwards, one of my older sisters, Philomena, eloped with her boyfriend leaving her baby at home, and I became even more insecure. I remember nights when my sisters and I would pretend to be talking to a man, signaling to potential attackers that we were protected. We called out the names of our brothers or cousins to create the impression that men were in our midst. It was a strategy my Mum employed when walking home alone late at night. She would talk at the top of her voice, pretending to be responding to her companion's questions. A flimsy trick, but it seemed to work.

We loved it when our maternal cousins stayed with us. We would feel safe in the presence of the young men, though we never told them this, not wanting their heads to grow too big.

Mum would also come home late at times, and I would worry about what might happen if she met evil people and they beat her up. This was a village with no lights: at six or seven in the evening, it gets dark and quickly turns pitch black. You could end up bumping into somebody without noticing them in front of you. Remember, there were no emergency services to call upon, nobody to come to your aid. We feared night attacks, we moved our belongings to avoid the rain, and we were the ones to do most of the household chores to keep our home going.

I lost sleep staring at the roof, listening for any movement outside. Nights were not happy and carefree, with no wishes for a good night or sweet dreams. My mother was a prayer warrior. Although she could not read or write, her knowledge and love of God were more than a formal school education could provide. Her prayers for us were far more than mere good night wishes; she believed God was the ultimate keeper, something I strongly believe, too. She believed that if someone wanted to harm us for no reason, God would prevent them from doing so. As both my parents abused alcohol, this led to some frightening incidents. Once, my mum came home with a section of a fence through her leg because she had fallen down on it when she was drunk, and she was bleeding profusely. My siblings and I wrapped her leg with clothes to try to reduce the bleeding overnight. With no overnight Accident and Emergency services, we prayed that she would survive to visit the hospital in the morning. Alcohol also intensified arguments between my parents; on one occasion, my dad chased my mum with a knife. She ran out to a neighbouring compound, and I followed her. It is likely that watching my parent's experiences with alcohol and the fact that alcohol is expected to have contributed to my dad's early death, strongly deterred me from alcohol.

Reflections on prayer at home

I must acknowledge that when my mother was sober, we had a regular practice of gathering in the evening to say our night prayers. This included saying the Hail Mary, The Lord's Prayer, and reciting the full Rosary. However, I must admit that I developed a dislike for the Rosary and secretly hoped my mother would not initiate it. The length of the Rosary and the requirement to go through all five stations made me sleepy and tired. Mum discovered my sleepiness from my lack of response when the prayers required one. Then, a kick or pinch would be administered to wake me up, which I did not appreciate at all at the time. Reflecting on those moments, I now recognize the need to seek forgiveness for my youthful perspective and limited understanding of God and prayer.

My mum asked a local chief to write a letter to the parish priest of Ichuni to take my sister Teresa and educate her because she could not. As you will see in the pages ahead, this is where all our blessings began. Teresa succeeded so well in education and rescued us all.

Our father, despite his exceptional intelligence during his school years, found himself falling behind, losing his excellent job as a town clerk due to alcohol abuse. He tried to fight the habit, but without a support system, he was alone in this struggle, and alcohol consumed him. He did not know how to stop. There is a point beyond which the damage from alcohol cannot be reversed. My Dad's life was cut short, and we had little knowledge on how to support him other than telling him, 'Stop drinking,' which he finally did around three or four years before his death. In the end, his health was severely affected, and his memory was like that of someone with dementia. During that era, mental well-being was not spoken about; it was a stigma or taboo. With no support or rehabilitation systems, Dad was alone in this battle. Sad but true.

On the other hand, we children were thoroughly annoyed with our parents, not understanding their depression and frustrations. They received no emotional support from us because our focus was to finish our education, get jobs, and rescue this family. We supported our parents with money for food and a proper family home, clothes, etc., but we did not understand their emotional needs or depression or the professional support that was needed.

In the case of our mum, her unwavering faith played a pivotal role in shaping her outlook on life. She extended equal measures of love and kindness to all she encountered, regardless of whether they were her own children or complete strangers. This remarkable ability to radiate compassion was one of my mum's core attributes and one that our village now remembers her by because her love for humanity shone. Indeed, God had answered my Mum's prayers and blessed her with a long life, as she lived to be ninety-two years old.

Family income

In caring for my younger siblings, Stella and Ken, and managing household duties, I developed resilience beyond my years. Despite the hardships, I grew stronger, learning to fend for myself and shoulder adult responsibilities.

We lacked the money to buy spare napkins, so I was left to figure out how to use what was available to change the baby I looked after while protecting him from danger. With scarce resources, creativity was vital. Using available materials, I cared for my nephew Lawrence, adapting towels as makeshift napkins. The process taught me resourcefulness, a trait that serves me well today. I remember my nephew having small towel napkins that we secured with safety pins. We washed the baby's napkins when they were dirty, but limited water was an issue. There was a saying that a baby's poo is like soap and that washing other things with nappies would result in them turning out very clean. What is 'clean'? In my childhood, 'clean' meant no stains; it did not necessarily mean no germs—we didn't know what germs were.

I also had to keep an eye on my younger siblings, especially Stella, before Ken joined us from Nakuru, where he had been living with Dad. This involved making sure that they had their meals on time. Occasionally, I had to decide what we were going to eat and then prepare it. These responsibilities were overwhelming, given I was only 9-10 years old. As I grew older, on some days, I took full responsibility for the home when Mum went to visit friends or relatives. There was nothing like a sweet sixteen for me or anything to celebrate turning eighteen or twenty-one. There were no milestones aside from the transition from primary to secondary school. Since I was at home with Mum most of the time, I learned to fend for myself and take up most of her roles.

My mum and her friends would take turns brewing a popular local beer called Busaa. When they were ready to sell it in the local pub (Ekerabu), I would be in charge of the home, looking after my young siblings. It was a natural thing to take responsibility without being asked.

The local pub (Ekerabu) was owned by a wealthy member of the community. This pub was located near Kisii Prison. Here, village women, my mum included, rented space and took turns making and selling Busaa. I am grateful that the owner allowed women to have a space to earn money, thus empowering them.

They used maize flour to make the beer. The flour would be mixed with water, fermented for five days, and then roasted and dried in the sun. This product is called Chinkara in the Kisii language. Afterwards, chinkara would be immersed in water, mixed with millet flour (obtained from grinding dry germinated millet, known as Ememera), and then fermented for four to five days in a big pot. The result would be a not-so-potent beer, but it would be filling and satisfying to drink. The men and women who brewed it made money to support their families. But my Mum was different. Though she made good beer by all accounts, she gave most of it away for free and sold the remainder on credit. Those who drank on credit never paid; neither did she make any effort to follow up nor demanded any payment. So, she used our maize, our money to grind it, our firewood to roast the flour, our effort and labour to fetch water and see the process through, only to give the product away for free. Mum's generosity cost us dearly.

Changaa: a homemade, potent illegal spirit

When I was a few years older and attending upper primary school, my dad lost his job. My mum struggled to pay my school fees and feed the family. My mum started making changaa to sell; this was a potent intoxicant beloved by Kenya's rural and urban poor, who sought a quick kick from maximum liquor at minimum price. The name changaa literally means 'kill me quick.' We made local brews and liquors for sale to raise money for my school fees and necessities such as soap and sugar. But

Mum, always generous and charitable, gave all or most of it away for free. Making, distributing, and selling changaa has never been legal in Kenya; therefore, raids by police on so-called changaa dens and distilleries have always been common. The owners of the dens, the sellers and the drinkers have often been arrested and charged. There are stampedes as men and women in various stages of intoxication attempt to evade arrest and court appearances. Yet, the business endures.

Not the best option to get us out of poverty, but Mum took the risk because she was desperate for money. Therefore, she involved us in the preparation of changaa, so we became her spirit-making assistants. Before I knew it, I had become an expert in the distillation of changaa from beginning to end.

The process of making changaa starts with taking dry maize to the electric power mill to grind it into maize flour. Next, the flour is mixed with water to make a paste of maize meal. This paste, wrapped in banana leaves as a lining, is stored in buckets or pots, and put into a hole dug in the homestead. The paste remains buried for about five days until it starts to ferment and turns sour. Then, the paste is fried in a big open steel pan or drum without oil until it dries and turns brown. One needs plenty of firewood for this process, and it was my duty to search out and gather enough firewood. For the paste to dry properly, enough heat had to be generated, and someone had to keep stoking the fire to keep the flame hot while another kept turning the paste so it could cook well. I kept adding the wood to the fire while Mum turned the paste with a huge spade. The spade and pan were borrowed because we did not have our own. The villagers lined up in turns for these special tools, and one had to book a turn so that one did not miss out when at the point of need.

When done, we would dry the fried pellets, known as chinkara, out in the sun. In the meantime, finger millet would be soaking in a porous sack. As the water drained out, the millet would germinate. The sprouts of finger millet acted as yeast. As soon as the sprouting started, we would put the millet in the sun to dry and then grind it into flour. We added this to the mixture to help leaven it and hasten the fermentation process.

Sukari Nguru

I still remember grinding millet, not only for beer but also to produce flour for brown ugali. When maize flour ran out, and we had not been to the posho (maize) mill. During my childhood, we used special stones to grind grains and produce flour. The process involved a large stone called 'orogena,' where we placed the grains, and a smaller stone named 'esio' that we used to press and grind the grains on the big stone, ultimately creating flour for making millet ugali.

Next, we mixed the dry fried corn pellets, the flour made from the finger millet, and several kilogrammes of brown sugar, otherwise called sukari nguru—100 percent unrefined sugar. This mixture was stored away for seven to ten days to ferment and grow in concentration.

After one week, the concentrated mixture is ready for distillation and condensation. This process of making changaa is shown in the diagram below. The spirit-making starts with placing a big pot full of the concentrated mixture at the bottom, that is pot 1. Above that was a second (middle) steel pot 2 with holes at the bottom for steam to come through, and then it condenses at the base of pot 3. Pot 3 is full of cold water and is placed on top. Inside the middle pot, pot 2 in the arrangement, a small, clean pot 4 was used to collect drops of the condensed liquid changaa, which drops from the base of pot 3, a clear Vodka-like spirit. The arrangement of the equipment and sealing ensured that steam would not escape and would be collected as the product alcohol.

Making Changaa

Pot (3): Filled with cold water. The bottom of this pot is very clean to collect droplets of beer condensed from the middle pot. When it heated, I would empty it three time using a cup before I would dismantle everything and harvest vodka.

Pot (2): This empty pot has holes at bottom to allow streams of alcohol from pot one. Pot (4) is a small clean pot (inside pot 2) that collects changaa for bottling later.

Pot (1): Large pot, heated by firewood, with the mixture, called omosuka, that will finally steam up and go through the distillation process to create the drink. The fire had to be kept burning throughout the whole process.

A fire was lit underneath Pot 1, and the mix would start boiling.

The cold water in the top pot (3) would, of course, heat up and would need to be emptied and refilled with cold water three times before the level of alcohol content was achieved.

Then, finally, we would reduce the fire and carefully remove the sealant, starting from the top. Then Pot 4, which had alcohol droplets, was removed, and the pure and natural spirit was bottled for sale. We recycled this process several times. Mum had told us that if we prepared 24 bottles of changaa and sold all of it, we would have enough money for school fees. I remember very well that a full bottle, the size of a wine bottle, would cost 10 shillings. This was a lot of money at the time. A customer would rarely buy a full bottle of Changaa for himself. If one did, the bottle would be shared among as many as four or even five friends and relatives. Most customers bought a glass, or half a glass and gulped it quickly with a face contorted in delicious agony.

Soon, there would be many drunk people in and around our homestead. But most gulped their portion and, fearing the police would raid the place or wanting to be closer to their homes when the drink kicked in, hurried away immediately.

Sometimes, the people we welcomed, thinking they were genuine customers, would turn out to be plain-clothed police officers or informers on intelligence-gathering missions. We would go to great lengths to conceal our product, digging holes in various parts of the compound to hide it. Mum had her own informers, who alerted her if police were in the vicinity. If they reported that the police were around or that an operation was imminent, all would be ordered to vacate the homestead immediately, and all traces of the manufacture or consumption of the drink would be hidden, destroyed, or thrown away. Of course, nobody, except for those who were already intoxicated, would linger around when the alarm was sounded. If the police found out where the spirit was hidden, they emptied the bottles and then arrested the sellers and any drinkers.

In pursuit of funding our education and basic needs, we took these risks by mastering the art of distilling this potent but illegal spirit. Observing our customers' behaviour under the influence provided eye-opening insights. Even as a youngster, I understood the consequences of tangling with the law and the ramifications of our hidden spirit being uncovered. Losing our liquor was a heavy blow, considering the time spent gathering maize, processing it, and collecting essentials. The journey from dried maize to bottled changaa spanned three weeks, demanding significant effort and cost. We had a reputation for producing exceptional changaa and busaa, yet I chose to abstain from these drinks—a decision that, in hindsight, proved wise.

While my mother worked at the coffee factory in Nyambera, near the cow slaughterhouse, she occasionally went with small bottles of homemade changaa to exchange for stolen meat. Sometimes, she sent me to do this using a bottle we called 'ebatira,' half the size of a standard wine bottle. The women would stand by the fence of the slaughterhouse, pretending to be bystanders while knowing the deal. The men slaughtering consumed alcohol, so they would throw the meat, unwrapped, onto the bare grass. I'd pick it up, throw the wine to them, and leave, never minding the perceived dirtiness of the ground. They would also fetch cow blood and poo from the small intestine in exchange for alcohol. At home, the cow blood was mixed with boiled milk and left for a few days, creating a thick, satisfying mixture to eat with ugali. This was a time when we obtained meat in exchange for alcohol, and sometimes, I was sent to the slaughterhouse to pick up meat. The men were essentially stealing the meat from the slaughterhouse, which was meant for distribution to the town. These memories of survival remain vivid, reminding me of the challenges we faced.

CHAPTER THREE
THE RIVER

We went to the river to collect water for drinking, as well as to wash our clothes and ourselves. People with livestock, like cows, took the animals to the river to drink. The river was also a place for social gatherings, especially for youngsters.

To get to the river from my house, we had to walk along the main road to town, then onto a narrow path ('Rikori' in Kisii) that led onto a broader path called 'Maendeleo,' meaning progress in Swahili. Another small path led off Maendeleo and across a wooden bridge, which was made of two logs laid across the river, topped with grass and soil, to make a bridge to cross over to a piped water source.

When it rained heavily, this bridge could be washed away. There were times when I went back home without water because either the bridge had been washed away or it was too risky to walk on. Thus, I always tried to go to the river before it rained.

There were always long queues at the Egetacho (a pipe) where we collected drinking water. People often cut the queue, using excuses such as their age to go before me, which meant

I had to wait much longer than I should have. Some people went to Egetacho to wash their clothes or their bodies instead of using river water. At times, people washed their utensils using water from this pipe, dumping all the food remains there, which led to a buildup of food where we collected drinking water.

Egetacho in February 2023

We never boiled our drinking water from the river. We believed that if it was colourless with no visible particles, it was good to drink. If we saw particles, we used a sieve to remove them, thinking that made the water clean. Whether our water came from the stream, river, or was collected from rainfall, we drank it all without a care in the world, oblivious to the fact that we risked contracting water-borne diseases such as bilharzia, a disease caused by parasitic worms, and diarrhea. We drew water from the river, took it home, and used it right away. Even if we had known about boiling water to kill germs, we would still have faced the choice between using firewood to cook our dinner or using it to boil water. The former would always win. I remember not lighting a fire when we were cold because I was saving the firewood for cooking; such was the choice we often faced: heat or eat?

Washing at the river

Sometimes, I showered at the river under a tree so that when I carried water home, I would not have to use it for a body wash. I had to be quick because there might be passers-by or naughty boys peeping if they discovered a girl was having a bath behind a thicket. If I saw or heard the grass moving, which hinted that there might be a snake, I would run away naked. When people brought cows to the river to drink, we would rush because the cows might attack us or chew our clothes.

Despite this, I enjoyed washing at the river, and I could use more water to wash myself properly. It was even better if I was with my best friend, Obutu; she would watch over me as I washed and dressed, and I did the same for her. When all was over and done, we headed home with our pails of water, having washed our clothes and bodies and fetched water, thus killing several birds with one stone.

I longed for the day when we would live in a house whose roof was made of iron or tin sheets and had gutters to harvest rainwater. People who lived in houses with metal roofs could collect rainwater. Our house, being thatched with grass, denied us this opportunity. We tried improvising with banana leaves as gutters, but the water was dirty and dark because of the soot from the fireplace and the lizard excrement from the lizards that lived on the thatched roof. It wasn't drinkable. Sometimes, we were lucky because a neighbour with a tin-roofed or iron sheet-roofed house (known as mabati) would allow us to harvest water from their gutters, but only after they had filled all their own containers.

Terror at the river

I will never forget the bad boys who often gathered at the river. The young boys had catapults and used them to shoot Sodom apple fruits at me for no reason. I always hurried to get to the main road, where I could join the people coming from town and walk with them. Whenever I went to the river, I prayed not to encounter those boys.

Amidst the challenging weather conditions that rendered the river bridge slippery and the torment from the boys, there were also the girls who mocked and bullied me on my way to and from the river. My tears during the circumcision procedure became a point of mockery. This caused me to lose friends, as nobody wanted to associate with someone who was a coward. Nobody, except Obutu, stood by my side.

The bridge I used during my childhood, pictured in 2023, now with slight enhancements.

We were separated when Obutu went to work for my sister, Teresa, in the far-off coastal city of Mombasa, but she was like family. Indeed, she continued to help our family by looking after my sister's daughter. I lost track of her when I left Kenya to study abroad and was shattered to learn she had passed away in 1999. I felt bad. It hurt because I did not know about her death at the time. I would have attended her funeral to pay my last respects, but I did not have the necessary papers when she passed, so I could not travel to Kenya. Obutu was my best childhood friend. She had been with me during my most trying times as a child. I have fond memories of us taking turns to cut each other's hair. Together, we learned how to care for ourselves and our young siblings.

Animals also visit to graze and drink the water. People would leave their clothes on the grass to dry. It was not uncommon for cows to try to eat the clothes. When this was spotted, everyone would run and try to tug the clothes free. The cow would fight back.

The river, pictured in 2023. You can see someone being helped to put the water on her head and a cow in the background while people are socialising in the far corner.

If we managed to get the clothes out of the cow's mouth, they were usually damaged and full of creases that never came out, even after ironing. There were fights between the owner of the cow and other people if the cow stepped on people's clean clothes or ate their clothes.

Upstream, people are washing their dirty clothes and sending the dirt downstream, whereas others, including cows, drink from and defecate in the river. I took this picture in February 2023, showing that not much has changed over the years.

Fights often erupted at the river over quite simple things, such as somebody jumping the queue or somebody murmuring something under their breath, which another person thought was an insult. The question, 'What did you say?' 'Naki gwateba?' would be asked, and before an answer came, somebody would throw water in another's face, and a fight would follow. Only Obutu stood by me. Only Obutu had my back. Taboo or not, she was a loyal friend to the end.

Fun at the river

Some people would just go to the river to socialise. We sometimes built a dam across the river to create a small pool that we used for swimming.

My brother Alex and I had memorable moments at the river. Before he moved to stay with Dad in Nakuru, Ken, Philomena, Alex, and I would be at home together. Teresa was away in boarding school, and Stella wasn't born yet. Alex and

I would splash in the river—we didn't know how to swim. It was risky. The water was dirty, and at times, we encountered snakes. The people washing their clothes upstream poured the dirty water back into the river. Livestock would walk into the river, leaving dung behind. When we left the water, our skins would be dry and rough, but, of course, we didn't think much about that or worry about creams and lotions. We didn't know they existed. I was fifty-four before I finally learned to swim.

Philomena didn't like us going to the river. So, Alex and I would have to sneak out of the compound. Of course, she would report us, and Mum would tell us off, usually as the family gathered for the evening meal. Philomena had a point. Not only was playing in the water risky but she was also left alone to do the chores children were supposed to help with. Still, whenever there was an opportunity, we snuck out again.

When we had a successful hunt, we were not told off when we arrived home. Alex would throw the bait in the river to catch fish, and I was in charge of carrying the fish. Alex also had a catapult, and we would go out to hunt birds. We would often cover quite some ground, starting from our small compound and going into the nearby coffee plantation but never straying far from the river. Sometimes, we would share the kill with Philomena, and, in turn, she wouldn't tell on us, but other times, we would refuse to share our birds with her as punishment for turning us in. Alex was resourceful and adventurous. He was my playmate until he went to live with my dad; when he was with me at the river, I would not be bullied.

The journey home from the river

If you don't get somebody to help put water on your head, you won't take a full container. Sometimes, if you are not friends, people just refuse to help.

As I carried heavy jugs of water on my head on the way home from the river, I would meet thirsty people coming from town. They would see the water and ask for a drink. I would tell them I had nothing to draw the water with. In response, they would produce cups, bowls, and even gourds and ask me to serve them. We were taught not to refuse our neighbours or even strangers a drink. If I gave one, I could not deny the next, but I ran the risk of going home with a half-empty pot or bucket. And when I allowed them to draw water, I just prayed that the cups dipping into my bucket were clean.

By the riverbank, all sorts of plants were to be found. There was a plant that produced a lather when squeezed, which we used as soap. We didn't consider whether the chemicals from this plant were safe; for us, foam equaled soap. Indeed, this substance produced a cleaner wash for our clothes than plain water. It came in handy when we didn't have soap. In those days, the best we had was a bar of soap, and even that was expensive.

CHAPTER FOUR
THE FOOD WE ATE

In my childhood, hunger wasn't just a fleeting feeling; it was a constant companion.

Food at home and the culture of borrowing (egieseri)

Food was scarce. Three meals a day? That was out of the question. We often lacked basic ingredients like sugar, vegetables, salt, and cooking oil to make food.

We rarely had decent food. Each morning, we'd start with a humble bowl of cornmeal porridge. Come evening, our table would feature ugali paired with green vegetables. There were days when ugali and vegetables were both our lunch and dinner. Ugali is a mixture of water and maize flour stirred and turned repeatedly over a fire until it hardens into a ball. While it is popular among the Abagusii and throughout Kenya, ugali, unlike rice, is not laced with spices, onions, salt, or oil. However, it fills the belly and fuels the body, especially for those accustomed to hard work.

I often went to school hungry. If I saw fruit on the way to school, during lunch or on the way back, I would pick it up and eat it. Many days, I got back home hungry and had nothing to eat. I would start looking for something to eat, such as bananas, potatoes, or green maize, and prepare some food for the family. Sugar, milk, and bread were hardly found in our house because we could not afford them. We had tea with milk and bread once a month if we were lucky. It was difficult for Mum and Dad to put a meal on the table because neither had proper jobs. Our breakfast at home was usually plain cornmeal porridge with no sugar. There were times when we didn't even have the cornmeal flour to make porridge. Any Kenyan would understand that unsweetened cornmeal porridge isn't just tasteless but also speaks volumes about a family's dire situation.

Without sugar, we would not drink tea. Sometimes, there was nothing to eat after lunchtime. I remember times when Mum would give me an empty glass and ask me to go to a neighbour and ask for some sugar, which we would return when we bought our own. There was no knowing when that would be. Sometimes, neighbours did bail us out, but other times, I returned with an empty glass because they had nothing to give. And there were times when we cooked whatever was available and ate it because we had to fill our stomachs. We would collect bananas or sweet potatoes to eat with porridge or with black tea if we were lucky to have sugar, even if there was no milk. We called tea without milk 'turungi.' A favourite meal of mine included sweet potatoes or bananas washed down with turungi.

Visiting grandmother

The one task I really enjoyed and looked forward to was visiting my grandmother, Salome Kemunto, in the village of Bogeka. It was lovely to go there and have a welcome break from home and the everyday chores. I loved the fact that Grandma loved me. However, the journey was daunting—a six-kilometre trek, long and lonely. I walked in fear of a dreadlocked lunatic who was rumoured to attack and kill people along the route. Despite the fear of meeting this alleged madman, I always looked forward to being sent to my grandmother's place and thank God, I never encountered him. Grandma was pure joy.

One of the things I liked most about visiting my grandma was that she used to have dry meat on sticks, just like kebabs, roasted next to the fireplace. She would make ugali, pull out this dry meat, and sprinkle salt on it. We used to sit around the fire and eat this delicious food with a cup of sour milk to drink. Oh, how I miss that meal. She would then send me back with plenty of food—sugarcane, bananas, guavas, vegetables, maize flour and sometimes egechieto, a local sour milk which was shaken into a smooth, yogurt-like mixture. Whenever I returned from my grandma's home, family members would check the food I had brought, much like kids rummaging through shopping bags. Since I could not carry the load on my head, Uncle Joseph Nyamao would kindly pay my fare for a matatu (delivery vans turned into public service vehicles) to Kisii town, from where I could walk home. Or, if we had agreed on a return time, somebody would come to meet me in Kisii town and help me carry the food home. My mum also had friends in some shops near the matatu stop in Kisii where I could leave some food while going home to fetch somebody to help carry the load on the final leg of the journey. A ride in a matatu was a godsend, but walking home from Kisii town was a struggle if I did not get help. Sometimes, I could ask a stranger going in my direction to help and give them a piece of fruit in return. Luckily for me, our house was close to the road, and strangers were willing to help.

My grandma passed away in 1979. We believe she was around 66 years old when she left us, which is a relatively early age for her to have departed. When Grandma dislocated her hip, she was admitted to Kisii General Hospital. There, confined to her bed and unable to walk, I would visit her, bringing food and changing her nappies. Changing and feeding my grandma was a soothing, gentle process, and we would chat while visiting time lasted. She enquired about Mum and encouraged me to plant vegetables. She died from complications related to the injury without the family getting to know what really went wrong. The memory of losing my beloved Kemunto, likely due to a lack of proper medical care, still saddens me deeply.

News that my grandma had passed on was broken to me at school. I was told by someone outside the school fence— perhaps it was Mum or my sister, Philomena. I remember the shock, the raw grief, and how I screamed in disbelief. It wasn't even the end of the school day when I heard.

To make matters worse, I was informed that Grandma had wanted to see me before she passed away, which hurt me deeply because I was not there, and I would never know what she wanted to tell me. People speculated that she might have wanted to tell me where she had kept her money—as banks weren't commonly used, people often buried their money in containers or bottles. But by the time we arrived, it was too late. Grandma had already left us. I consider it a blessing that she wanted to see me as she lay on her deathbed. She used to call me Kerenchina, which is how she pronounced the name Regina. It still hurts that I was not there to hear her last words.

Grandma and I shared a unique bond. We never argued. She had a way of mentoring me. I wish my grandmum had lived to see my success. She would have been the happiest grandmum around. She had a golden heart that I was always drawn to. She was generous, and I was always grateful to receive gifts from her. I have learned so much from her. Just like her, I try to have the same spirit of generosity. She truly blessed me, and I like to imagine I, in turn, can pass those blessings on to those around me.

God appointed her to watch over me and took her too early, but I believe I will meet her in my next life.

Malnutrition and disease

Despite occasional supplies from Grandma, we suffered from malnutrition as children, as well as waterborne diseases and skin infections. After eating, it was common for me to experience stomach pains due to worms, but I was never able to pinpoint the cause of the pain. The lack of knowledge prevented me from seeking treatments. For the lice in my clothes and hair, Mum resorted to using strong pesticides, the kind meant for coffee farms—clearly not meant for human use due to their harsh chemicals. Chigoe fleas, we knew as Jiggers invaded and burrowed themselves into our toes, getting under our toenails, between our toes, on our toes, and on our heels. I can hardly believe the variety of parasites that my body was a host for. We removed the parasites by carefully peeling back the skin, using a needle or a safety pin to remove the whole parasite without breaking it to avoid leaving eggs in my toes. If those tools were unavailable, we used a strong thorn. We would pick them out whole and burn them in the fire, enjoying the popping sound they made. After removing them, we sometimes placed a drop of kerosene or tick pesticide in the gaping holes left behind. The idea was that kerosene or pesticides would destroy any eggs left behind and stop the reproduction of the pests.

The lice laid tiny eggs all over my clothes. What an embarrassment I suffered. I would be seated or standing among friends, and a lice would appear on my forehead. We washed the bedding with pesticide, too. Despite everything, I always tried to look my best.

Mum had dogs and cats, which were never treated and were likely carrying diseases. As for the hens, if they were sick, we would crush some herbs the villagers believed to be medicine and feed them. We grabbed them one by one in the morning or evening, opened their beaks, and poured medicine.

These pictures of me are from 1981, aged nineteen and in Form Two, i.e. the second year of secondary school this in Nyabururu church compound after Sunday mass.

Food scarcity

There were times, however, when there was absolutely nothing to eat, and I would crave even a piece of sugarcane. A piece may have cost ten cents, but I could not lay my hands on a five-cent coin. On such days, I would wander near the road close to my home. I sometimes saw a chewed and discarded piece of sugarcane. Sometimes, it was covered with ants, but sometimes, I would be lucky enough to find fresh ones that were not yet attacked by the ants, and I would eat them.

The hunger I endured during that time is something I never want to experience again—the weakness in the limbs that I wouldn't wish on anyone. Unfortunately, hunger still plagues the world.

On the rare days when there was tasty food, and Mum was around, she prepared goat ribs in her favourite earthen pot called 'Egetega' (a fragile pot made from clay.

Egetega'

The resulting meal was always delicious and would put us all in good spirits, delighted and excited. When Mum cooked meat, she did it slowly and expertly. We always enjoyed her food.

Pooling resources in the village economy

There was always a lot of work to do in our compound, including tending the maize, beans, cabbage, bananas, and fruit trees and keeping the compound and house clean. The maize had to be weeded twice a season, with soil gathered around each plant, or it wouldn't produce a good harvest. The women of the village would form groups and weed, in turn, the crops of one of their number until they had done it for all their members. We didn't benefit from this effort because Mum did not join the groups, opting to hire people as a one-off and giving them food and traditional beer as payment. But most of the time, she lacked these resources. Although our piece of land was small, we often failed to weed our maize and coffee crops a second time, which meant our harvests were not good. This is something our parents should have organised but were reluctant to do so. To counter this, we children and our friends formed social groups, known as egesangio, to help our mothers complete a second weeding.

We were all about ten to twelve years old, and we would dig the land and weed for each member of our group. We formed these groups and moved together from one homestead to the next, weeding the maize until each member of the group had benefited from our collective labour. We enjoyed doing this in the evenings after school, especially when there was no rain.

In some ways, we, the children, became our parents' parents. We were the ones who were organised. We worked out what labour was needed and attended to it at the right time. We looked out for weeds and kept our house and compound clean and tidy. It meant, in many ways, that we were adults early and missed the milestones that many kids remember with fond memories. We didn't acknowledge becoming teenagers, turning sweet sixteen, or even becoming legal adults. We were too busy caring for our families.

CHAPTER FIVE

CHRISTMAS

Christmas Day was the one annual occasion when we could count on enjoying exceptional food. We longed for Christmas because we knew that our tummies would be full.

It was well worth the wait because we would have tea with sugar and mandazi (deep-fried and raised buns) for breakfast before leaving for church. Christmas lunch at home consisted of beef or chicken stew with ugali or chapati. If we were lucky, we would have Treetop, an orange squash, or soda. After Christmas lunch, we would line up to be served the juice in cups, followed by a dessert of ripe bananas.

In our young minds, Christmas meant food. It's not that we didn't appreciate the significance or the celebratory side of Christmas. It's just that food, or the lack of it, dominated our thoughts on so many occasions.

Preparations

Preparations started early. We decorated the outside of the house first; we would plaster our mud-walled houses with coats of clay. The clay was held together by cow dung—if you didn't have cattle, you could ask neighbours for dung. After the first coat of ordinary clay had dried, we used murram, yellow clay called 'ekebuse' in Kisii, for the decorative coats. Girls were responsible for finding a quarry with ekebuse, mining it, taking it home, mixing it with water and cow dung, and plastering it on the walls, which were allocated to the girls.

I did all this with my friend, Obutu, working on our houses until we were happy with the results. To get the best clay, we first had to excavate the stones at the quarries, which were around two kilometres from our homes. We needed to get to the fine dust that lay beneath the stones. As we dug deeper, we widened the hole so that we could fit inside it with enough space for digging, fetching, and moving the clay with relative ease. The deeper we went in, the riskier it became. Accidents did happen. The walls caved in, and the miners, often children like us, were trapped and died under the weight of soil and rocks. I lived in fear of such a tragedy happening to us.

It was demanding work but also delightful to carry out as part of the preparation for Christmas, possibly the only time of the year we knew we would eat well. Of course, we knew Christmas was not just about food, but when you've barely eaten, you might find that food often occupies your thoughts.

Nyambera Quarry: as a child, I would climb down into the crevice as shown in the middle of the picture to mine ekebuse.

The house walls were smeared with murram soil from the quarry ready for Christmas.

*Carrying harvested maize home or to the power mill ("posho") was
a must-do during my childhood, like the young girl above.*

*One of my daily responsibilities was gathering firewood from
the bushes for cooking, like the child in the photo above.*

It was risky and tiring carrying these tasks. Sometimes, when I took the heavy load of clay down from my head to rest, I would rely on passers-by to help me put it back on my head. If it started raining while I was resting on my way home from quarry, the clay on the ground would become even heavier as it absorbed water. If no passers-by came by to help lift it back on my head, I would have to run home without it and start the journey again the following day. Often, I would wait in the pouring rain of a tropical thunderstorm, out in the open and not seeking shelter under a tree, for fear of being struck by lightning.

We also decorated the inside of the home. Starting with the bare walls, we caked them with clay and improvised our decorations. Much of this took the form of drawings with a banana pen—a peeled, fresh green banana, held like a pen—which we used to create our own unique Christmas 'graffiti' on the inside walls. I liked to draw flowers, but we could draw anything, including silly pictures of family members. Decorating the house, inside and out, was the task of us youngsters, and we loved every minute of it.

In addition to banana scribbling, we bunched up old newspapers to make decorative shapes on the walls to hang, as shown in the picture on next page.

Most of the year, we couldn't afford rice, so it was lovely to have it on Christmas Day with chicken. We would pick a chicken for the pot, usually the largest one—the rooster. With some tomatoes and fried onions, it made a perfect soup.

Finally, we needed to make sure we had sugar for our tea. We went most of the year without sugar, but we saved up enough money to have sugar on Christmas day.

Inside the house, newspapers used to be used for decoration. This was in my uncle's house.

Then, we had to turn our attention to the compound. Everything had to be clean and neat for the big day. With my dad and brothers away, this work fell on me. I would make sure the grass was mowed and the hedges were cut. I would sweep around the house to ensure everything was tidy and welcoming for Christmas.

The day itself

The first thing we considered was when to go to church. Nobody wanted to go during the day because it was dedicated to eating the delicious food we had prepared. That meant everyone preferred the midnight mass. After mass, we walked home singing Christmas carols, eager to get home to delicious fried dumplings washed down with sugar-sweetened tea.

Then, the next morning, we would get ready for our lunch. We would lay the table and give thanks for the scrumptious feast of chicken soup, rice, and ugali. There was little money left for presents. One year, I remember receiving new underwear for Christmas, little boxer shorts. As a child, I was happy to play hop, skip, and jump, so my dress rode up to display my new boxers underneath to my friends. I was content with my gift.

A sad Christmas

One Christmas, we returned from night mass to find our house broken into. We were horrified to see that our chickens and our store of fried dumplings had been stolen. This was utter misery for us. Imagine all that anticipation followed by such disappointment. We had to turn to our neighbours for whatever food they could spare. They were kind to us, but it was not quite the same thing.

That was the last time we went to midnight mass. The following year, we decided to stay home and guard the compound rather than make the journey to church. That was a great pity because the joy of mass at night was simply wonderful, with candles and wishes of Merry Christmas all around.

CHAPTER SIX

PRIMARY SCHOOL

I was in primary school from the age of 8 until I was 17. Many children in the village did not go to school, simply because they couldn't afford to. For most, the decision came down to a stark choice: food on the table or books and school fees. So, it's not surprising that food won. Even when opportunities to go to school arose, parents, many of whom had not been to school themselves, preferred to give their sons a chance rather than their daughters. The common belief was that girls would be married and take the benefits of their education to their married homes rather than helping their original family. If resources were stretched, a boy would go to school while his sisters stayed home. Girls suffered severe discrimination, but nobody complained because that was the norm within the culture. The belief that girls would marry and leave to their new family, taking with them the benefits of education, while boys would remain at home, was another consideration that never favoured girls.

If a girl married and the husband started abusing her, it was hard for the girl to run back home. Most fathers would say, "Go back to your husband." Fathers, having used her dowry for her brothers' marriages or other purposes, would often send her back to avoid giving back the dowry. As a result, many women continued to stay with their abusive husbands.

Children from a few lucky families in our village were sent to school. At least our parents could just about afford primary school education with support from our first-born sister, Teresa, and income from the traditional beer changaa I made. With my parents, education was for all of us, not just boys.

I looked forward to school because, even at a tender age, I could see it offered a way out of the extreme poverty we endured. Education meant an opportunity for me. As we shall see, it presented enormous challenges and involved extra hardships, but my future would have looked bleak without the education. I persevered through those struggles.

Nyambera Primary School

Despite the scarcity at home, my parents were willing to send me to school, something I'm grateful for to this day. I considered myself extremely lucky when I was sent to a nearby school called Nyambera Primary to start Class One at age 8. I was older than my classmates.

Though the primary school was nearby, the journey was difficult. I followed offroad tracks enclosed by thorny bushes and slippery mud underfoot. If there was heavy rain, the route would turn into a river, making the journey impossible. There were even times I encountered my biggest fear, snakes, along the way.

If I fell and returned home because my uniform was muddy and wet, I would be caned by the teacher the following day. Teachers did not accept excuses for missing school. The teachers had the freedom to cane pupils as much as they saw fit, depending on what a child had done. We would be caned if we were late to class after break, even if we were in the toilet. There were teachers known for their extremely painful lashes; you never wanted to be sent to them for punishment. These fully grown adults used all their energy to flog young children under the guise of discipline.

Even with the hardships, such as sometimes going to school without breakfast and usually not having lunch, I enjoyed going to school. I was excited about learning new things and meeting my friends. Occasionally, I carried left-over ugali from the previous night, and one of my school friends brought in cooked beans or milk in a bottle, and we shared our lunch.

We even studied farming, which I was familiar with due to helping my family grow crops. In school, we created a section in the classroom that we called a 'nature corner,' where we planted beans, maize, and flowers. We nicknamed the runner bean, 'Jack and the Beanstalk.'

School also offered me a break from the heavy workload at home. However, I quickly learned that nothing would be so easy. At Nyambera Primary School, we were expected to clean the toilets, pick up rubbish in the compound, weed the flower beds and sweep the classrooms, which was not very different from the chores at home. Cleaning the toilets (pit latrines), in particular, was not a fun task.

During the dry season, our classroom would be filled with dust. To tackle this, we split into groups: some of us would head to the nearby river to fetch water for sprinkling on the classroom floor, reducing the dust for sweeping, while others cleaned up the school playgrounds and the teachers' quarters. These tasks were our early lessons in responsibility and teamwork. However, fetching water was a dreadful task. The water came from a stream which was contaminated by human excrement dumped into the river upstream by Kisii prison inmates. Additionally, the water was polluted by drainage from Kisii Mortuary. As kids, we were unaware of these grim realities. This was normal, and it was all we knew.

I didn't have an exercise book for each subject. I used one book to write all the notes for every subject and used the same book for my homework. It was difficult to get a pencil. I only had one. I would cut mine into two pieces, using one at school and keeping the other safe at home.

In 1971, when I was just nine years old, my nephew Lawrence was born. I was in standard 2 when my mother took me out of school to help babysit Lawrence so my sister Philomena could return to her studies. My education was put on hold to care for her child. The rationale was that Philomena, being older, could finish school sooner and eventually start work to support the entire family. However, after one year of returning to school, she eloped with her boyfriend, leaving the baby with us, and didn't return home. The decision to take me out of school really affected my progress. At seventeen, I was in primary school when I should have been in high school.

Switching schools

After babysitting my nephew for two years, it was time for me to go back to school. Teresa transferred me from Nyambera Primary School to Kisii Primary School. This was a prestigious school in Kisii town, managed by the Municipal Council. I was excited about the new school and determined to make a difference in my life and change my circumstances for the better. I was 12 years old when I returned to school in 1974, with five more years ahead to reach standard 7. I completed primary education at the age of 17.

Teresa has always been one of my greatest sources of inspiration. I admired how she carried herself and the many things she did to help our family situation. I admired the uniform she wore when she visited with her friends from school. Nyaboke is her African name (meaning honey). I remember running to meet her as soon as I saw her coming home, singing and shouting joyfully, 'Nyaboke omito ochire' (translated as 'Our Nyaboke has come'). She was like our saviour.

Life in my new school was different from Nyambera Primary. Here, children wore shoes with socks, sweaters, and jumpers as part of the uniform. Most of the parents worked either as teachers or as employees of the municipality, plus there were other formal or informal employment opportunities in town. The children appeared neat and smartly dressed in their uniforms. At Kisii Primary, the emphasis was on learning, with minimum manual work for the students. The school even had piped water; it was a true blessing to be able to concentrate on learning.

We were expected to arrive at school before 7 am for the morning preparatory class. This meant I had to wake up early, prepare myself and walk the two kilometres to school. There was no electricity or even an alarm clock; I relied on being woken up by the sounds of birds or roosters at daybreak at about five o'clock; they sounded again at around six, and I knew it was time to get up.

This is the table, and the kerosene lamp (ekebeya) I used for studies. My eyes itched from using the lamp because it emitted lots of smoke. After some time, if I blew my nose, it would be full of soot.

As the oldest in my class, I was appointed as a class prefect and ultimately as head girl. This meant, unlike other pupils, I was exempted from tasks like occasionally picking up rubbish in the school compound. Instead, I was tasked with maintaining discipline in the classroom when the teacher was absent. Due to this, some pupils called me names, and the nickname I hated most was Mama Kelele, which is Swahili for 'Madam Noise' or 'Noisy Mama' or, literally, 'Mother Noise.'

I had very few friends in primary school due to being elected prefect. I was often tormented by other pupils. I remember some boys kicking my backside with their shoes, lifting my clothes, exposing me from behind and showing my underwear in town. It was very embarrassing.

Menstruation

Another thing that would confine me to my class was my period. As I was older than other students, I got my period before other girls. I had no sanitary products. I had to reuse pieces of blankets as pads. Money was tight, so I had to reuse the same blanket scraps monthly. There were no new blankets to cut into pieces every month. During school, I would rather sit and not go to play because exercise would increase the flow. I was constantly worried, especially when the flow was heavy. I also hoped not to be sent to the staffroom if my dress was stained. I only had one uniform dress. If it became stained, my discomfort increased, and I didn't want people to have another reason to bully me. However, I was still expected to move back and forth from classroom to staffroom, whether to pick up new materials for the teacher, collect forgotten books upon her/him arrival, or acquire new textbooks, chalks for the lesson and keep order in class.

Back home in the evening, I would wash off any stains and hold my uniform close to the fire to dry it while being careful not to burn it. I could not press it because we didn't have an iron. We didn't have running water in the house, so I cleaned the dress using a cup of water. When going to school, I'd have another piece of blanket nearby.

After a total of nine years, I successfully completed my primary school education with two grade A's and a B at the age of 17, qualifying for entry to a good secondary school.

CHAPTER SEVEN

SECONDARY SCHOOL EDUCATION

After I completed primary school, I was admitted to Nyanchwa Secondary School, a Seventh Day Adventist (SDA) establishment. Like most secondary schools in Kenya at the time, it was a boarding school. I was excited by the prospect of moving out of the village and hoped my experience at secondary school would be better than at primary school.

Well, there was absolutely no peace for me at Nyanchwa; conditions just got tougher. I was not at all happy with my new school. From Friday evening on, there was a great deal of time devoted to church. We were immersed in singing and Bible studies until late Saturday. This was done in celebration of the Sabbath. Then, on Sunday, we spent most of the day doing manual work.

I was not a Seventh-Day Adventist, but all students had to abide by SDA religious practices. As a Catholic, Sunday was supposed to be my day of worship and rest. I asked my sister, Teresa, to find me a Catholic school because I couldn't adapt to the routine of SDA. I didn't mind the Bible studies; it was just the long hours that exhausted me.

Nyabururu Girl's Secondary School

Luckily, Teresa was working as a deputy headmistress and contacted Sister Margaret Bradbury, the headmistress of Nyabururu Girl's Secondary School, a Catholic school. Teresa managed to get me a place in Nyabururu, and I swapped my SDA school for the Catholic one in the second term.

None of the schools I attended in Kenya served sufficient meals. Meals at Nyabururu Girl's High School were small and tasteless. Most students depended on their pocket money to supplement their diet. That meant that after dinner, before evening prep, students would send passers-by to buy them bread, soda, sugar, or Milo (a chocolate drink). The strangers would pass the snacks across the fence, as they were not allowed into the school compound.

There were no electric kettles in the dormitories, so girls would fill their thermos flasks with hot water from the school kitchen at dinner time. They would then brew themselves tea or hot chocolate after prep. Even getting the hot water was a struggle because, sometimes, the cooks didn't have enough of it to prepare the meals. Also, trying to get hot water if the cooks disliked you was quite a challenge. I had to force myself to smile for the cooks when I wanted hot water. Sometimes, I had sugar, milk, tea bags or even hot chocolate, but I couldn't use them because I couldn't get any hot water. At times, I had the luxury of squash, but the lack of water meant I couldn't even dilute it. The situation in the dorms was even worse;

the water wasn't fit for drinking, yet we had no choice but to drink it.

A thermos flask was a luxury item that would save me from starving, but I couldn't afford one. I watched and suffered in silence as other students had tea and bread or squash, a mixture of oranges and other fruits, before going to bed after 10 o'clock.

Sometimes, the cooks didn't prepare enough food, and some students missed out on their dinner because there just wasn't enough to go around. Life for the poorer ones was bad on Sundays when we went to church because some students would be brought food by their parents or relatives. After the church service, I'd try to make friends with such students, but when they got their food, they all went to eat with their other friends.

The hunger that ate at my stomach weakened me physically but strengthened me mentally. With every passing day, I grew more determined and more resolved to create a better life for myself and my family.

I had to keep up with the school routine like any other student. I still went for prep to study for the following day's classes; even as a young girl, I saw this as a way out of poverty. I would check my homework, make sure I revised my lessons and be ready for each school day. Studying on an empty stomach was normal. I worked harder so that I could eventually always have food on the table.

Visiting Day

The most miserable days of my secondary school life were visiting days, which were the best days for most students. This was a day for home-cooked food: my classmates' parents brought them chapati and other treats. Parents and relatives of other girls visited them frequently. During my four years at Nyabururu, my sister Philomena visited me once, and Mum came once when I was sick. I felt sad and alone every Sunday. What were days of joy and reunion for my schoolmates were days of solitude amidst hunger pains for me.

On the designated visiting day, students were allowed visitors in the dormitories. People would eat and play music there. It wasn't ideal for me to be in the dorms on such occasions, as I had neither food nor visitors. I would either stay in the classrooms or sit somewhere under a tree, continuing with my revision while others took their visitors to the dorms. It was hard for those of us who did not have visitors to see friends eating, but we understood that these were family occasions.

There was one good thing about visiting day. When the bell for lunch rang, people with visitors did not turn up in the dining hall due to the poor quality of food being served and they now had good food from home. The absence of students meant their food would be shared among fewer people. So, on visiting days, there was a chance my portion would be bigger than usual.

After lunch, my friend and I went back to the far end of the compound, where, under the trees and on our bedcover spread on the grass, we resumed our reading, revision, or homework. Since nobody came to visit us, we would read and ask each other questions from the chapters we were studying. Some of the teachers were housed in the school, so we prepared questions and waited. If we saw one of the teachers heading to the staffroom or coming out of it, we would approach them and ask our questions. We invested our time well when our classmates were enjoying family time. The work we put in during the weekends really rewarded us during the week.

But the visiting day did not end when the visitors left. The torment continued into the night after prep. Students whose parents had been visited tucked into their delicacies once more. The smell of chapati, fried dumplings, bread, hot chocolate, and other aromas filled the air in the dorms. The hunger would become intense before I eventually dozed off. Many of my dreams, inevitably, were about food.

Sourcing water at secondary school

Students arrived at school armed with buckets and basins. We fetched water from a nearby stream if the piped water supply was disrupted, and kept it in the dorms under our beds as we went to evening preps. Prefects and our seniors would often sneak into the dorms at prep time to steal our water we collected for washing. It was frustrating to return to your room after evening studies only to find that the water you collected was stolen. If the person who took your water had some remorse, they might leave you a bit of water.

But this was never enough for a bath. It was just enough to enable me to use a flannel to clean my body in the morning. Sometimes, if all your water had been taken, other students were kind enough to share a cup of water.

Sick in school

One day, I fell sick and was permitted by my class teachers to seek treatment at the Kisii General Hospital. I was also desperate to visit my mother and see if I could get some food back with me to school. So, I wore my home clothes first and then my uniform on top of them on my way to the hospital. Once outside the school compound, I shed my uniform in a bush. That way, if I encountered any of the nuns or priests, they wouldn't know I was a student out of school.

All I wanted was to get home, be greeted by Mum, receive some food, and then visit the hospital for treatment. I was very sick at school and so desperate to see my Mum too, hoping and praying to find her at home. But tragedy awaited me; Mum was not at home. My heart sank. Sick, tired, hungry, weak, empty-handed, and penniless, I staggered back to the hospital and then to school. I regretted asking for permission to go to the hospital. In my tired and weak state, I had to gather all the strength I could to walk over four miles back to school via the hospital. I couldn't even skip the hospital visit because, upon returning to school, I needed to prove to the matron and teachers that I had indeed been treated by showing them a hospital ticket in my name.

I couldn't drag my feet and rest awhile by the side of the road because if I missed dinner at school, I would go to bed hungry. Usually, when students went out of the school compound for one reason or another, they returned late, armed with food and some pocket money. I returned late and nearly missed my dinner. I was sick and without money for the fare to and from the hospital. I was too weak to walk, yet somehow, I had to get back to school. Sick and tired, weak and lonely, everything seemed to be stacking up against me. Had things been different and Mum had been home, I would have had food to eat and feel better, but now I felt even sicker. Perhaps I would have bought myself a bottle of Treetop and showed off my dinner of a loaf of bread and butter in the dorm that evening. I would have arrived at school happy, despite my sickness.

That night, I cried for a long time. I wondered if there was a reason for me to be in school and to be pushed so hard and with so little given in return; it was one of my lowest moments in school.

Snacks

One of the types of food I would take to school at the start of term was 'Chinkara,' a form of fermented cornmeal dough left to dry in the sun. It saved me many times when I was hungry. I just added cold or hot water to it, and the meal was ready to eat. Sometimes, I would add sugar, but this was rare because sugar was beyond my means most of the time. Chinkara is used to make traditional beer known as 'busa' and was banned in school, but we sneaked it in all the time.

I was talking to a friend one night in 2022. She's now living in America. We were classmates at Nyabururu, and we talked about the terrible hunger we endured in school, revising with an empty stomach. She recalled how we would go to the top end of the school compound and sit there reading because we didn't want to be anywhere near the entrance where we would see parents and relatives coming in to visit other students. We knew they were bringing them food, drinks, love, and warmth. She reminded me of how we longed to be visited but knew we were hoping against hope. She reminisced how she picked up the remains of banana skins to scrape the flesh. In reply, I told her how I chewed sugar cane from the streets, which had been chewed and thrown away by others. We thanked God that we have both come a long way.

I was at Nyaburu for four years and successfully completed my ordinary level (O-Level) education, passing the national exams for entry to high school at the advanced level (A-level).

The next stage in my long educational journey loomed, and I was ready for it. I looked forward to when I would complete my education and make it in life. Although I faced challenges at all levels of my education, I knew it was the only chance I had to change my life. I finally completed secondary school and moved on to high school at the age of twenty-one.

CHAPTER EIGHT

HIGH SCHOOL

This picture was taken in 1984 with my classmates at Mukumu Girls on the opening day of sixth form. I'm in front on the right carrying an iron box on my head and a small suitcase in my left hand. We have just alighted from a bus at the school main gate, entering the compound.

I celebrated my third major academic milestone when I was admitted to Mukumu Girl's High School in 1984. The two-hour journey to my new school took me through the districts of Homa Bay, Kisumu, and Vihiga before we got to the school, which was in Kakamega. This was my first long trip away from my home district of Kisii. I was excited about going to sixth form because I was going to study science subjects, which would allow me to study medicine at university. My sister Teresa gave me money for the fare, paid for my shopping, and ensured I had the basics demanded of a student going to a new school, such as a complete set of uniforms.

Joining high school was a privilege. Many girls during my time did not go beyond Form Four, the final year of secondary school. A sizeable number of them ended their studies at O level at 16 years because their families lacked the money to take them to high school. Most of them got married or became primary school teachers. I was, therefore, extremely lucky that my sister Teresa was willing to pay my school fees at Mukumu Girl's High School. She appreciated the value of education and encouraged me to go on. I knew I was fortunate, and I am still grateful today for Teresa's vision and generosity.

My trip started in Keroka, Kisii, 25.5 kilometres from Kisii town. The matatus (minibuses) used for transportation were crowded with passengers, making it an uncomfortable journey. Students were often asked to crouch, kneel, or stand to accommodate adults as the vehicle travelled to Kisii town.

Once in Kisii, I disembarked, retrieved my steel suitcase and other belongings from the luggage rack, and searched for a matatu heading to Kisumu. At each stop, I had to hurriedly locate the matatu going in my direction, which was not straightforward for later trips, as the location of the bus stops frequently changed. Carrying my suitcase on my head and holding my hand luggage, I squeezed into the crowded matatus.

The matatu conductors loudly announced the destinations their vehicles were heading to at various stages. They would urge passengers to hurry up and board before it became fully packed; when my direction was called, I would rush there to board. The conductors were often kind, taking my suitcase off my head and throwing it up onto the roof of the matatu and strapping it quickly before the vehicle moved off.

The stretch from Kisii to Kisumu covered 106.6 kilometres and was a long and uncomfortable ride as the vehicle was overloaded and extremely crowded. In Kisumu, it was time to disembark and find the matatu for Mukumu. Usually, they were bound for Kakamega, the principal town of the then-Western Province. With most schools opening on the same day, they would pick up students headed to Kakamega first, meaning a long wait in Kisumu. Eventually, a vehicle would be heading to Mukumu, and many of us would clamber on board.

The final section of the route covered 40.2 kilometres, the final stage of a journey that began in the morning and ended late in the afternoon. My suitcase was packed solid, with clothes, books, food, shopping for three months, toiletries, and cutlery. It made for a heavy case to lug about between matatu rides.

Life in Mukumu was difficult, partly because I wasn't doing the right subjects. My sister and I, like most Africans, believed that if you are not studying medicine, law or engineering, your degree is just not good enough. I, therefore, cast aside all the subjects in which I did well in my O-level exams and started battling with physics and chemistry. I aimed to prepare myself for a degree course in medicine at the University of Nairobi. After two years of studying, I failed my exams and was not accepted to university. I should have stuck with the subjects I was good at, but I didn't receive any such career advice.

Struggles at Mukumu Girls High School

On top of my struggles with my subjects, my social life at Mukumu High School was just as difficult, mainly because I had no pocket money. I struggled financially most of the time, lacking the money I needed to support myself. At Mukumu, I was only given KSh20 (£0.11) as pocket money per term.

At school, we had our lectures and the usual prep in the evening. Sometimes, students also went for morning prep. The challenges I faced throughout the school term revolved around food. Yet again, there was not enough food, but I was expected to study and concentrate on what the teachers said. How can somebody study on an empty stomach? This theme of constant hunger is a thread that runs through my entire schooling experience and indeed, my entire childhood.

There was a man at Mukumu High who supplied food to the school canteen, and the students who had money would ask him to bring them bread and drinks. In the evening, as we went to the dormitories to prepare for night prep, the girls would pass by the school shop after supper and give him money to buy food. The driver would bring the food when he delivered supplies to the canteen. My KSh20 pocket money for the whole term was not enough, even for cotton wool, which I used as pads for my periods. After prep, the girls settled down to eat something because they were hungry. I was hungry too, but I had nothing to eat.

These memories will never leave me because they made me work hard at every chance or opportunity that came my way; they are part of who I am now. I love to help others because I received so little help myself.

Memory of this hunger, a constant throughout my childhood and student days, will stay with me forever. Hunger and fear were my two constant childhood companions. The hunger dates back to my very first days on this earth. But in Mukumu Girls School, hunger made it impossible to meet the expectations to excel in and pass science subjects with minimal food to fuel my body and mind, as evident in my final results. I failed flat and left that school without any qualifications.

Motivation to Succeed at Mukumu High

After evening prep, from 7 pm to 9 pm, students ran to the bathrooms for extra studies. The dormitories had no lights at this late hour. Unlike other areas of the school, there was light in the bathrooms, but there was also a terrible smell from the unclean toilets. One would book a place to sit and study until about 1 am. This was a good school, and one needed to perform well to get into a fine institution such as the University of Nairobi. That was my aim at the time.

Everybody at my high school worked hard for their futures, to make something of their lives, none harder than me. When I consider how it was then, I see that those students back in Kenya were dedicated to their studies for the sake of their futures. I didn't have any snacks, but I had to study, or I'd fail the exams.

Again, in the morning, I would wake, shower, comb my hair, dress, and run for morning prep for one hour, followed by breakfast. We read non-stop to pass examinations and hoped to find our way to independent, fulfilling lives.

After breakfast, we attended the assembly and then had classes until lunch break. At lunchtime, the food was not enough and not often particularly tasty. Inevitably, we went to class in the afternoon, still feeling hungry. It was not until after the first two lessons that I managed to forget about the hunger and seriously focus on my studies. Then, it was time for games, after which we ran to the dorms, rested, showered, and got ready for dinner. Small portions again. There were rumours that the portions were made small on purpose, allegedly to motivate students to work harder. But those who had money had backup food in their dormitories, which they ate after prep. My take is that if the food given to us were adequate, there would be no need for food after prep. Students resorted to buying food because what was available in the school kitchen was little and often tasteless.

Results Day

But much as I read like mad, I failed my exams flat. How was I supposed to achieve anything in these conditions, battling subjects I wasn't comfortable with, having no money and very little to eat? My time at Mukumu remains the saddest of my long journey in search of knowledge.

I entertained the thought that I was a stupid girl, but, really, I was not. Those around me failed to see the issues I was going through; one can be with people and yet feel entirely alone. This should never happen with education. Students from disadvantaged backgrounds demonstrate incredible resilience by working tirelessly despite having empty stomachs. Sometimes, I faced additional hardships, like falling ill at school. I was often left in the dormitory sick while my peers attended classes; nobody seemed to realise that poor nourishment and long hours of studying would inevitably take their toll. If I was lucky, when ill, a matron might provide medicine and water but no extra food or real comfort, both of which can be as healing as any medicine.

Sometimes, students didn't improve and got worse. And it would be only one person, the matron, doing the rounds.

Resitting A-level exams at Nyabururu Girls

I was going to give myself another chance to go to university. Even though I failed, I believed I was capable. So, I returned to Nyabururu in 1987 to repeat Form 6. I had been there from 1980 to 1984.

Once again, my education was delayed. This time, after failing my exams, I had to take an additional year to resit. I was now the oldest student in my class by far. I joined Mukumu for my A Levels at twenty-three. This was very late already. Many students would be graduating from university at twenty-four. I was almost the same age as some of my teachers. I finally completed high school at the age of 26 years.

Mukumu shared several similarities with Nyabururu. Both were sponsored by the Catholic Church. Both were adjacent to convents and headed by Catholic nuns. The difference was that Mukumu was further from home. I immersed myself in my studies as I had done in my previous school. However, the hunger and food situation was worse at Mukumu than at Nyabururu. The visiting days at high school were difficult for me: not a single person visited me, and my loneliness was worse than at Nyabururu.

After retaking the school years, I managed to get five points at A-Level. This wasn't enough to study medicine at the University of Nairobi as I had hoped. I was devastated after all the years of schooling. It was then that my nephew, Lawrence, saw a newspaper advert calling for applications for scholarships to study in Poland. We were sitting outside the house when he came to me and said, 'Auntie, why don't you apply for this?' He handed the paper to me. It called for applications for scholarships to study pharmacy in Poland. I applied, thinking it would be glamorous and fun to study in Europe. In fact, the destination was later changed to Morocco by the Ministry of Education.

I was stressed out before this scholarship opportunity came my way. I was thinking about diploma courses, teaching jobs, buying a camera, becoming a photographer, or even going into commercial farming. I lost a lot of weight worrying about my future now that the route to university looked blocked.

I could have taken law at Nairobi University if I had pursued the subjects that I did well in for my 'O' levels, but I was pushed to Mukumu Girls' high school to do triple science subjects to get into the school of Medicine at Nairobi.

Reflections on secondary education

Education was my way to the future. It was the route out of excruciating poverty and for my life journey.

The harsh conditions of my childhood forced me to adopt different strategies for my survival. I had to. Apart from going to school hungry and being the oldest in my class, I shouldered heavy responsibilities at home, forcing me to learn life skills to survive. I often compare myself to a cactus tree, which cancapable of withstanding all seasons.

Ashamed of my age and size because I had been out of school to look after my nephew, I would put my head down to try and not feel different from everyone else in the class, but the young ones bullied me and called me names. Bullying was another hurdle I had to overcome to achieve a better life. I was nearly an adult for much of my latter years at school. There were no options to study with other adults, no choice but to put on the uniform and attend school.

Given the amount of manual work I still had to do at home when I returned from school, I had to plan my time carefully. I studied and did my homework at night using a kerosene lamp. This wasn't easy because our house did not have proper windows. I needed to open the door to allow more light in and the smoke from the lamp to go out, but I could not open the door at night until around 5 o'clock in the morning when I woke up to do a bit of revision before school time. Fear filled my stomach until daylight fully broke. I lived in constant dread of being attacked by lurking dangers, a fear that haunted me every day in those early hours.

Watching the daybreak was always a wonderful feeling. I always felt that I had gone through the worst and, therefore, the future was bright. We did our studies in the living room. There were no carpets or laminated flooring, just a soil floor. No heating, no plumbing, no running water. The table on which I did my studies was low, and so was the tree stump that served as my chair. I would bend low so that I could read and write. This sitting position was far from comfortable, but it was the only way.

I remember my Mum sending me to get her a plate for ugali when she was cooking. In the dark, I couldn't tell the clean plates from the used ones. Mum was using the firelight to check on the cooking. I brought the plates close to the fireplace to differentiate the clean ones from the dirty ones.

The sense of deprivation was truly profound in my life in many ways.

CHAPTER NINE

LIFE IN A CATHOLIC CHURCH MISSION

I was nineteen and in Form Two when the Reverend Nicholas Oucho accepted my sister Teresa's request to take our parents in because they had fallen on tough times. The legacy of Father Oucho, a Luhya by tribe, is that of a selfless priest who led by example. The compassion, commitment and love he preached at mass at his Ichuni Parish in Keroka and at the many centres he set up throughout Kisii, will stay with me forever. He helped families in need. He built schools and churches. He paid fees for the children of parishioners, and he mentored young men and women who sought the priesthood and sisterhood, respectively. He made Keroka his new home and Abagusii, his community. Education and the word of God were his be-all-and-end-all.

Father Oucho was a tall, dark-skinned man of God who changed the lives of my family. First, by paying Teresa's education fees and, second, by accepting Teresa's plea to accommodate my parents in his Parish, providing them with secure housing and care, he saved them, and the rest of us, from poverty.

Teresa was just one of the many girls for whom Father Oucho paid school fees and provided residence at the mission. Those girls hailed from many parts of the country. Father Oucho welcomed all and served all who came to him equally.

Although I was already in boarding school, I did not immediately like the idea of relocating to the mission as it meant leaving behind my friend, Obutu. When the school closed for the holidays, I would now head from Nyabururu Girls' High School to Ichuni Mission, which was located near Keroka town, rather than going to our home village, which was closer to Kisii town. Father Oucho was like our guardian, and he granted my sister the use of a house in the mission so that she could support us from there. Life started getting better for us.

I felt safer in the mission than I did in the village. I didn't have to think about security at night. I didn't have to think about going to the river to fetch water or getting firewood from the bush. I didn't have to think about light for my studies, as there was electricity in the mission and, if there was an outage, the priest had pressure lamps on standby. I was no longer going to be facing the local boys who bullied and beat me at the river when I went to fetch water.

However, there were negatives as well. I had lost all my childhood friends, and yet we had not moved too far away. When I was young, a short distance, like from Keroka to Kisii town, felt like miles and miles away. It also bothered me that our sleeping arrangements were separate. Stella was accommodated in the staff quarters where Mum and Dad were, and Ken was with the boys in their quarters. This means we were never together under one roof as a family at night.

Starting to make new friends is difficult when you live in a mission. You cannot go out as you please and do what you want to do as a young person. I spent most of the time with my friend, Yulita, a girl from Tanzania, who was being supported at the Ichuni Parish. Yulita and I slept in the dormitories because the servant quarters were small. When students were away, Yulita and I would have the whole dormitory to ourselves. Imagine two young women alone in a large hall meant for thirty-five. It felt strange and empty.

Mum used to go back home to Nyankongo to see her friends and relatives. She would seek permission for two to three days but would end up staying there for three weeks. After greeting and spending time with her friends at Nyankongo, she would proceed to her late sister's place in Geteri and later to her original home, Nyakoe, to visit her orphaned nephews and nieces. Initially, I was annoyed because she was gone for long periods, but looking back now, I would have done the same in her shoes.

While my Mum was away, fear and anxiety ruled us. We wondered if we would be told that she had been killed or found dead because the places she visited were not safe. At times when Mum was away, Dad suffered fits.

But nobody thought about how this affected the siblings, Stella, Ken, and me. Similarly, nobody realised that Mum was distressed because all her brothers and her only sister had passed away, except for the youngest brother. She had no emotional support. She had food, a roof over her head, and a compound to live within that provided all the essential amenities, but the human soul needs its own amenities and basics for survival. It was hard for Stella and me as we took care of Dad. Teresa would be teaching while Stella and I looked after Dad.

Reflections on life in the mission

It later dawned on me that Dad and Mum faced extreme boredom in the mission. They had no work, no responsibility, and nothing to look forward to. They were miserable, which is why Mum would seek permission from the priest to leave for three days and be gone for weeks.

During our childhood, my siblings and I were unaware of our mother's depression and its underlying causes. Mental health issues, including depression, were not widely understood or discussed back then, which often led to reactions of frustration or anger when we couldn't comprehend what she was going through. We were simply limited by our knowledge and understanding at that time.

Now that I have children of my own, I have gained insight and empathy towards my mother's situation. If this happened now, I would approach the situation with more compassion and understanding, as I've learnt that mental health issues can have a profound impact on individuals and their relationships. It is disheartening to know that even today, there remains a need for more robust support systems when it comes to mental health.

As I reflect on the past, I acknowledge that my knowledge of mental health issues, depression, and loneliness was non-existent, and there were no support systems available as there are today. My concept of support primarily revolved around ensuring my parents had access to food, medical care, and necessities like clothing.

There were other emotions at play here. As their children, we also became frustrated and disillusioned. For instance, I never did what normal teenagers do, like meeting my friends to get food, do activities, or just have enough time to chat. It's important for the young ones to go out and mix with others so that they can learn from each other—not just classroom skills but gaining social skills and becoming streetwise. It's something I'm having to learn now, making up for what I couldn't learn back then.

Yulita attended Uganda Martyrs' Secondary School, also known as Ichuni Girls' Secondary School, and she worked for the priest as an altar server. She arranged the priest's clothes on Sundays and weekdays. At some point, the priest asked me to accompany Yulita and learn how to prepare the altar. Yulita taught me how to carry out the daily chores of the church and, importantly, those at the altar. Occasionally, we read the weekly readings during church services. Being selected by

Father Oucho for reading was both an honor and a nerve-wracking experience.

The priest went out to other centres occasionally, so we had to pack his suitcase with the sacraments, wine, cups, and clothes—all that he needed to carry out mass, including the baskets for offerings. These shared responsibilities brought Yulita and me closer together, and we quickly became best friends. Hunger was a constant companion for us, and sometimes, particularly on Sundays, after counting the offerings and taking the money to the bank in Keroka, we'd discreetly keep a small amount, about KSh5 (around £0.03 at today's exchange rate) and buy ourselves something to eat. It was usually sugar and bread. We ate the bread as we walked back to the mission. Yulita was good at making chapati, so when schools opened, and I would be leaving for Mukumu, she always made them for me. Unfortunately, we lost contact, and I have not seen or heard from Yulita in many years.

If the local boys knew that two young girls were sleeping in that huge dorm alone, we could have been attacked or even raped. Such thoughts were scary, but thank God, a guard named Sakwa guarded the place. His presence assured us that there was security.

However, I felt ashamed that I would come from boarding school to sleep in a dormitory. I felt that I lacked a proper home. I wished we had a different place to go to. I never invited my friends over because we lived in a mission. I never experienced any of the things that teenage girls do, like having sleepovers at their friends' places or birthday parties. I did not have permission to entertain friends in the mission. This may sound as if I am ungrateful, but I will be forever thankful for Father Oucho's support for my family. I also appreciate that it is hard for the priest to take on a whole family, feeding them and all that comes with it.

Staying in the mission put a strain on my family. Away from home, we all depended on Teresa's income from teaching. We all missed the familiar faces of our community back home. My parents were unable to provide for us. My dad suffered from a condition in which he would become confused for 2-3 days following convulsions or seizures, with what I now believe to be early-onset dementia. Sometimes, he would not remember his way back home.

Father Oucho never knew that the cook was a mean woman who hid and ate all the decent food with her sisters. In fact, the sisters' presence at group breakfast, for example, was only a pretense, as they would have already eaten well. They had a full breakfast of tea, eggs, bacon, bread, cereals, and fruit. Mum, being a staunch Catholic, believed that people ultimately get what they deserve for their wrongdoings. She did not bother to report the cook to the priest. Eventually, Father realized the situation in the kitchen, and he started giving each person bread daily. We each received a weekly kilo of sugar, a ration I would never have dreamed of before.

When Teresa transferred from Mombassa to Lwanga Secondary School in Ichuni, our life as a family improved significantly. She was an angel. She could have chosen to go and teach in a school far away from home and forget about us, as many young people opted to do, but she chose to come home for us. Our whole family owes a lot to Teresa and Father Oucho. Teresa led by example, and we followed. She worked hard and helped us, which taught us to take our endeavours seriously and turn to each other for support and strength. I think all of us have done exactly that, and the family is on a different path now.

Mum, the village elder.

After 17 years in the mission, my family went back home to Nyankongo after my father died in 1997. My family built a new home for my mother and relocated her from the mission in Keroka. This was a permanent house. It was now possible to trap water from the roof, and there was no need to go to the river if it rained. When I returned home from Britain in 1999, I sat outside where our grass-thatched house once stood and remembered how much Mum had prayed for her family.

It was during this time that Mum was appointed a village elder and was later promoted to senior village elder, assisting Chief Zachary Ondieki Onchuru in the administration of our area. Chief Onchuru told me that my mother was his advisor and oversaw Nyankongo, which had a population of about two thousand. He also reported that my Mum used to accompany him to his meetings, known as baraza, and other functions in the location. She was an advisor in the community and helped solve disputes among the local people. The former Assistant Chief of the area, Ondieki, described Mum as an intelligent leader who could solve the community's problems with fortitude. Ondieki said he relied on Mum's support as she held court in the village for several years.

My first job

In Kenya, my only job after completing Form 6 was working as an untrained teacher at a secondary school named Nyaturago in Keroka, Kisii. I earned a salary of less than £10 a month, which was still enough to buy groceries. Our cultural practice is to contribute to the family's needs when you earn. As a result, I used the little money I made to buy things for my parents and family without anyone telling me to do so. I can vividly recall purchasing a large tin of cooking oil and sugar, which had to last us for a month. Despite these efforts, my pocket was often empty, and lunchtime was a challenge. The school was in a remote area with no shops, except for those selling soda and bread and locals selling ripe bananas and sugar cane by the road. We had a staff room where teachers pooled money for lunch and tea. Lunch was just simple but kept us going, consisting of ugali and kale, known as sukuma wiki, meaning 'push the week'.

This photo captures a rare, close moment with my dad, it was taken in Mombasa's Rabai Mpya, where my sister Teresa taught. around 1979. From left to right: The little girl in white is Jacqueline, my cousin Patricia's daughter, next to her is Lawrence, my nephew, my sister Philomen's son. Top left is my sister Teresa, followed by me, then my dad William, then my brother Alex. On the second row, the little girl in front of me and Teresa is Teresa's daughter, Cynthia. Below Cynthia is my sister Philomen's daughter, Jacqueline.

PART II:

FROM KENYA TO MOROCCO, MOROCCO TO ENGLAND

CHAPTER TEN

THE SCHOLARSHIP THAT CHANGED MY LIFE

My first trip to Nairobi, the capital of Kenya, was when I was 26 years old. Someone had come to me with a letter. It was a letter with my name on the front. It was a telegram letter from the ministry of education Nairobi. It bore a life-changing message in response to my scholarship application:

'You have been offered a scholarship to study Pharmacy in Poland. You are instructed to report to the Ministry of Education at Jogoo House, Nairobi, for more information.'

I turned the note repeatedly. 'Me? Nairobi? Pharmacy? Poland? I could not take it all in at once. I was ecstatic. I read it three times…four times… until it began to sink in. My head was in the clouds. I was going to Poland! Europe! I was going to fly! An aeroplane! My sister's voice brought me back to earth and the present. 'Now you must go to Nairobi,' Teresa congratulated me. She was just as full of happiness and excitement as I was.

In 1988, I set off for the first time from my rural home on the life-changing journey to Nairobi in search of more information about my scholarship.

I had made many trips from my village to school and to my grandma, but all of them were in Kisii. I had visited several schools in Kisii and made the more than 200-kilometre-long journey to Mukumu for my high school several times. Therefore, by local standards, I was well-travelled. But I had not been to Nairobi, the capital, although I had been to Mombasa on a day school trip from Mukumu Girls High, but that was it. The journey from Kisii to Nairobi takes about six hours by bus.

I was absorbed by the scenic views of the countryside. I felt like I was travelling to another country, as the safari seemed to go on forever. It was a sort of culture shock as we crossed the neighbouring districts (now counties) because I did not know much about Kenya. In those days, the main route from Kisii to Nairobi was through Kericho and Nakuru. I didn't have a watch, so I didn't know when we left. I was keen to read the names of the towns and landmarks along the way.

After about twenty minutes from my home, we entered an area where I noticed vast tracts of land with old-fashioned English houses and well-manicured compounds. 'Where is this?' I asked my seatmate on the bus.

'This area was formerly occupied by the white settlers. It's a highland area. When they left, some locals bought the homes, and it came to be known as a settlement scheme,' came the answer.

There were Ayrshire and Friesian cattle breeds in the compounds. I had only seen such cows in textbooks. My villagers did not keep such grand cows. 'These residents must be having a lot of milk,' I said, to which my seatmate nodded in agreement.

Within the hour, we crossed the river Kipsonoi, which marks the boundary between Kisii and Bomet counties near Sotik. Soon, the bus was climbing through an area that looked more like a piece of art than real. I saw an endless, tabular, lush green crop that meandered through the hilly terrain on both sides of the road.

Litein tea plantation in Kenya

'What is that?' I asked my seatmate again.

'This is a tea plantation, Litein, the man next to me answered, adding that there were many more similar tea estates. He sounded quite knowledgeable about the route. 'This is amazing!' I exclaimed.

A certain warmth jolted my heart. I had never seen anything as beautiful as this. God blessed me on this trip. At the time, I didn't know the significance of this place to me as the homeland of my first love, William Ngeno, the father of my son.

Even my village, where it rains almost daily, isn't as beautiful as the tea plantations. The tea estates in Kericho rolled out like huge carpets punctuated by rows of tin-roofed huts that served as staff quarters. This is where my dad also worked, albeit for a brief time.

Soon, we were entering Nakuru, the principal town in the expansive Rift Valley region, where we would stop for a lunch break. We crossed the railway line, and I saw a train! I wished I had a camera. The train honked and snaked around the station in the opposite direction. Next to the station, I saw a Kenya Pyrethrum Board sign. The pyrethrum plant is grown in Kenya as a cash crop. Nakuru was a small, clean town halfway between Nairobi and Kisii.

Under normal circumstances, students would have travelled to Nairobi at least once or twice in early childhood, either as part of school academic tours or to visit relatives. This wasn't the case for me. I thought it was magnificent when I saw the pink colours of the flamingos making patterns on Lake Nakuru. I felt like running out to touch the water of Lake Elementeita and would have done so had the bus stopped.

Pink colours of the flamingos making patterns on Lake Nakuru

At Naivasha, I saw herds of stunning zebras and majestic giraffes catwalking along the road. For the first time, I saw the sun setting from the highest point of the escarpment overlooking the Great Rift Valley, one of the most iconic landscapes in Africa. It was the most breathtaking view I had ever seen.

I saw the majestic, massive cactus trees around Kijabe. At that moment, I was simply captivated by their natural beauty, not knowing that later in life, I would establish a profound parallel between the resilience of the cactus trees, which maintain their vitality even amidst the harshest droughts, and my own journey.

Zebras grazing at Lake Nakuru

Wildebeest resting at Lake Nakuru

Great Rift Valley Cactus trees near Kijabe

This trip left me with a long-lasting impression of my country. Yet I had no idea how big my country's reputation was among foreigners until I got to London. I found online advertisements for safaris and excursions to Kenya, where people save up to witness incredible experiences. They travel to Kenya to see the famous Big Five animals and witness the breathtaking wildebeest migration across the Mara River. I began to appreciate why they saved money to travel to Africa to see wildlife. I understood it when I met people who were saving to make what they regarded as a lifetime safari to Kenya.

Arrival in the capital

I dreaded encountering the City of Nairobi after disembarking from the bus. I had been told that my cousin, Tumbo, stayed in Nairobi West and that I could find transport, but I had no idea where I was going. Relying on the goodwill of strangers at the downtown bus station for directions, I finally got to the house at around 8.00 pm. My cousin offered me accommodation during the short stay while I followed up on my scholarship. Someone from the household who knew the city well would take me to the offices of the Ministry of Education in the morning. I didn't even know how to use the road crossings to go when the green man indicated.

The following day, my cousin Regina, who shares my name and is Tumbo's sister, took me to the ministry's headquarters at Jogoo House in the Central Business District, located on the famous Harambee Avenue. This avenue is home to the Office of the President and Deputy President (the two of which are these days called the Presidency), the National Treasury, the Police Headquarters, the Attorney General's Chambers and the Ministry of Foreign and Diaspora Affairs. This was my first time in a high-rise building, and it was my first time using a lift. Of course, I had to be taught how to operate it. My cousin then showed me which bus to use to get back to her home. I joined the queue of people waiting to see the Minister for Education.

It was my turn to go in when his secretary informed us that it was lunchtime and the minister was going out. We were asked to return after the lunch break. I was apprehensive about leaving the office to go and look for lunch because I was afraid that I would get lost or come back late. Therefore, I decided not to break for lunch and to wait for the office workers to return. Remember, I had no watch and thus could not tell the time. Navigating the city was a challenge for me because it was difficult to get my bearings. Crossing city roads was a nightmare, and there were just too many cars. This made it difficult for me to explore the city despite my desire to do so.

During my afternoon interview, I was given forms to fill out, with the clarification that I was to go to Morocco, not Poland. The change in the details did not affect my overwhelming joy.

My relatives in Nairobi West were not as excited about my scholarship in Morocco as I was, perhaps because they didn't see Morocco as prestigious as a European country. But nobody would dampen my excitement because I wanted that degree badly and had earned the scholarship. In any case, I had failed to gain admission to the University of Nairobi, and there was no chance that the situation would change.

I was required to make several visits to the ministry to complete the paperwork. My main challenge during these visits was that I did not have money for lunch and would, therefore, go hungry the whole day. This would then force me to run to the kitchen immediately after I got back to my cousin's house. I was embarrassed because it was not my home, and I should have waited patiently until dinner time.

I went back to Kisii after two or three weeks. Then, I got a letter from the ministry saying that my scholarship had been confirmed and I needed to collect travel details. I then made another trip to Nairobi to make the final arrangements for my journey to Morocco.

As I celebrated my scholarship, I was confronted with a new challenge. I needed to raise money for my airfare. I travelled back to Nairobi and went to the office of the Member of Parliament for my Nyaribari Masaba constituency. Professor Samson Ongeri listened carefully as I explained my case. I needed his assistance to enable me to raise money to buy my air ticket to study in Morocco. I had a scholarship, and I showed him the evidence. Ongeri asked me to return to his office the following day. I naively thought he would give me the money when I got into his office and joined the considerable number of people waiting to see him. When he appeared, he said: 'You people have come all the way from Kisii to ask me to find you jobs as sweepers of Nairobi's streets. Let me see this child who is seeking to go and study abroad first.' I was so flattered that a legislator and professor had acknowledged my achievement.

Ongeri took me out of the queue and led me to his boardroom. He had gathered several MPs from Kisii to raise the money for my ticket. I could hardly believe it. In a matter of minutes, I had raised enough for the ticket, and I was overjoyed. He asked me whether there was anything else that I required, and I said no. I felt I had received more than I had expected or hoped for. I couldn't believe that he had not only accepted my request for partial assistance in raising the funds, but he also took the initiative to organise a fundraiser for me at such short notice. I had the whole amount I required for my ticket. My heart was bursting with happiness. A heavy load had been lifted from my shoulders, but I could not share the great news with anyone because I did not have a phone to call home.

Ongeri and the MPs advised me to work hard in my studies, advice which I noted, and it's been hard work, hard work till now, and it paid. In 2021, I spoke to Ongeri by telephone and thanked him from the bottom of my heart. I was reminded at home about the time he stepped in and helped me. I still plan to see him and shake hands with him. I pray to God to make this happen. I told Ongeri I worked hard, as he and other Kisii MPs had advised me.

It was at the scholarship office elevator that I crossed paths with William. He was accompanied by his father while I was alone. William asked me where my scholarship was going to be, and I shared that I was headed to Morocco. He was scheduled to fly out to Morocco the next day. Little did I know that he would become so important in my life.

During the time that I stayed with my cousin's family, public transport in Nairobi was efficient. Traffic lights worked as they should. Pedestrian paths were clearly marked, and the flower beds were well maintained. Still, I did not venture out much. I was afraid of the big city. I never got to enjoy the serenity of Uhuru Park. I was a stranger in my capital city right up to the time I left Kenya.

Here I was, coming from the village at twenty-six years old and behaving like a child on her first day out. I was moved to tears when I saw some children being shown around by their families. I came across groups of school children on tours. Though I did not have someone from my family to show me around, I cherished what Cousin Regina had done in guiding me to the ministry and the bus stop. All of it helped me overcome my fear of cities.

Winning the scholarship made me think I was at the pinnacle of achievement. As events turned out, I'd just taken the first few steps on my journey, one that was fraught with trouble and difficulty.

My trip to Nairobi was filled with challenges. I had no money, was unfamiliar with the city, and had no one to guide me. However, it ultimately transformed into a journey of blessings, shaping me into the person I am today. My life was just beginning. I am grateful to God for all the blessings I now enjoy, and I give Him the glory for them. It turned out to be a blessed struggle.

CHAPTER ELEVEN

LIFE IN MOROCCO

I left Kenya for Morocco on 1st November 1988. As I embarked on my first solo journey, a mix of thrill and uncertainty coursed through me. The prospect of navigating foreign lands alone was both daunting and exciting. However, amidst the tornado of emotions, there was a comforting thought. Having crossed paths with William Ngeno at the scholarship office in Nairobi, I had a glimmer of hope that I might encounter a familiar face in Morocco. William had travelled there a day earlier.

As the plane soared above the clouds across Africa. I marvelled at the landmarks I had studied in geography, from the river Nile to the Sahara Desert. I spent my time on the plane gazing out of the window, captivated by the scenery passing below me. I was filled with excitement. When I arrived in Rome on a layover, I sent a postcard to my sister Teresa, which felt like a surreal milestone. It was hard for me to fathom that I was in Europe and so far away from home. I was due to travel from Rome to Rabat the next day.

Arriving in Rabat, my heart skipped a beat as I spotted William's face among the strangers. I felt grateful that God had sent me a companion in this foreign land. Joined by a group of Kenyan students who had already been studying in Morrocco, I felt a sense of belonging wash over me. Over time, we all became a tight-knit family.

Before I started my medicine course, from 1988 to 1989, I went to the Faculté des Sciences de l'Education to study French. After that, I attended the Université Hassan II de Casablanca to study medicine in French. William went to the École Nationale Supérieure de l'Administration in Rabat. William and I visited each other on the weekends and developed a strong friendship. Soon, it became more than friendship, and we started dating.

A picture of Willy and me on Avenue Mohammed V in Rabat in 1989

Our monthly stipend, or 'buss' as they called it, was only 550 Dirhams (£43). During the holidays, all Kenyan students in Morocco stayed together in a house in Rabat because renting apartments individually was expensive. We pooled our resources to afford rent and food. I contributed 200 Dirhams for rent, and the remaining 350 Dirhams were barely enough to live on. Most of the time, I was either hungry or had just enough food to get by from day to day.

However, as the second year progressed, our struggles intensified, and we battled sickness due to our lack of proper nourishment, which left us physically weak. Despite that, our spirits remained strong. Deep within, I held onto the belief that a miracle was on the horizon. I had faith that God would send an angel and that sunny days were ahead for us.

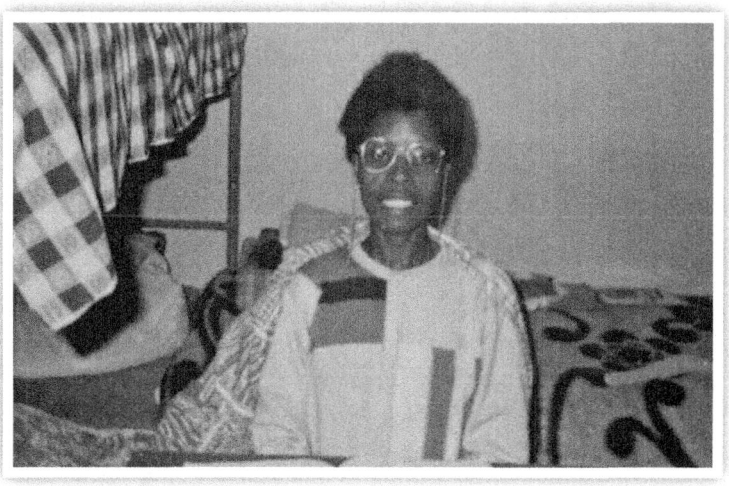

This photograph shows how I was severely underweight during my time at Université Hassan II in Casablanca.

In 1990, my health began to decline rapidly; the above haunting photo of me, taken by my roommate, became a poignant symbol of the harsh realities I faced. On a bleak day, I asked for this picture not as a snapshot but because, in my heart, I feared it could be a potential final image for my family. During those times, my thoughts often returned to my experiences of hunger throughout my childhood. Separated from my boyfriend in Rabat, I pressed on in my unwavering pursuit of education. I wrote several letters home but never received any responses.

In Rabat 1990- These are the times I will remember as blessed struggles. My ribcage bones could be counted as I was severely underweight during my time at university.

In the summer of 1990, I faced my biggest challenge yet. I became pregnant. When I found out and told Willy, we went back to our room, shocked, and looked at each other. I remember Willy pointing towards the brown bath towel we owned and saying, 'We will use that towel for our baby'. And that was it. We never regretted keeping our baby, but it was really tough.

The prospect of having a baby was daunting. We had no savings. We were receiving only £43 each per month, which wasn't enough to sustain us, let alone a child on top of that. It was difficult to see a way forward. Every night and every day, I was gripped with worry. Part of me was grateful that God had blessed me with a child, but most of me couldn't understand how we would survive. I was a foreign student in a new country and pregnant during my second year. I found myself overwhelmed by helplessness and surrounded by what seemed like insurmountable roadblocks.

During the Gulf War, the American Embassy advised students to take precautions or leave Morocco. For us, this was even more important because of the baby. With only $50 in my purse and pregnant, I left for England while William planned to travel to Spain to work in the farms, picking apples and oranges, to generate an income for us. I have learned from these experiences that when one comes to a point where one can't go any further, God steps in to rescue you. It was at this moment that the fear began to dissipate.

CHAPTER TWELVE

EXIT MOROCCO,
ENTER GREAT BRITAIN

Despite the turmoil of having to leave Morocco, an opportunity to go to England was far better than returning to Kenya empty-handed. I was pregnant with no qualifications, and my family had high hopes for me, anticipating that my success abroad would help alleviate poverty within the family.

It's remarkable how global events can reshape individual lives in ways we never imagined. The urgency and importance of our decision to leave Morocco were heightened by the imminent arrival of our child, adding a deeply personal dimension to our story.

Why England? Pure chance is the answer. Father Joseph Morris, an American priest in Kenya, told me about a Kenyan called Mairura living in Nottingham, England. They knew each other from missionary work in Kenya and had become friends. My sister Teresa had also introduced me to Father Joseph back in Kenya. We were a family dependent on the mercy of the church. I wrote to Mairura in Nottingham, asking him how I could get student jobs in England while on holiday, and he told me there were no student jobs in England, but I was welcome to visit. So, I set off for England, arriving at Joseph Mairura's home in Nottingham on 11th November 1990.

It turned out that Mairura's mother was my sister Stella's godmother, making it a small world indeed. This coincidence gave me great hope that they might assist me in staying in England and remaining in their house. After a while, Mairura's wife realised that I was pregnant. She advised me to return to Kenya, arguing that I could not possibly survive in England without money and being pregnant, as there were no job opportunities for students. Instead, I headed to London to join another Kenyan student Viola who had travelled with me from from Morrocco. I then joined the Bible Way Church. The church and congregation helped me greatly, giving me food, clothes, and shelter.

In this photograph taken in 1990, I'm wearing two dresses for warmth. These dresses were donated by church members.

I recall a lady from the church community, leaning out of her 5th or 6th-floor window, requesting her husband, who was going shopping, to "bring more milk for Sister Regina," referring to me and my unborn baby. Their compassion truly felt like a blessing from God.

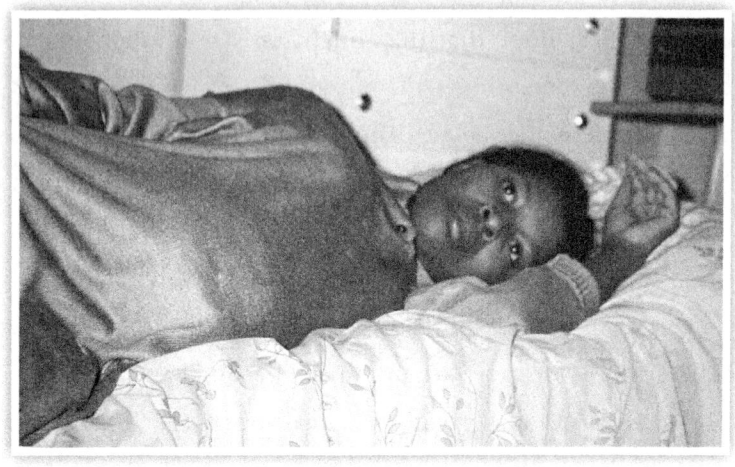

In this picture from 1990, 7 months pregnant,
I was overwhelmed with fear and naivety.

I was uncertain about how my growing baby was being sustained, even without the essential nourishment I yearned for, such as monkey nuts and pears. Unfortunately, affording these simple luxuries was well beyond my means. Even a glass of milk felt like an unusual luxury while residing in someone else's home. As a result, my diet remained basic despite being pregnant, as I endeavoured to blend in like everyone else.

During this time, William, unknown to me, arrived at Heathrow to join me, but he did not know that I had moved away from the host family in Nottingham. I was writing letters to him in Morrocco, but he had already left for Spain. Without phones, we couldn't connect, and I had moved to London.

Given three days by immigration officers at the airport to locate me, he was unable to, leading to his deportation back to Kenya. When I found out about this, the realization hit me hard, knowing that our reunion had been thwarted. His return home, full of frustration, only compounded the despair I felt upon learning about the situation. The weight of the news, coupled with the impending arrival of our baby, left me feeling isolated.

My anxiety escalated as I recalled the challenging experiences my sisters faced with caesarean sections. The thought of undergoing this operation without any family support was a source of great fear. The concern about managing the pain loomed heavily over me. When labour failed to progress naturally, and the child couldn't emerge due to the cord around his neck, the only viable option was a caesarean.

I was totally dependent on the church, and they were generous and kind to the extreme. This help continued when my baby was born in April 1991.

He entered the world weighing 8.12 pounds—an indication that he would have been a huge baby if I had access to better nourishment.

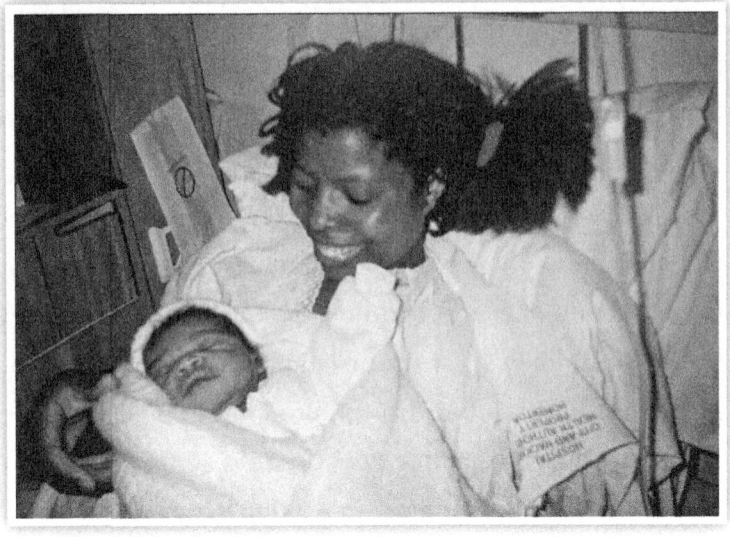

The birth of baby Emmanuel in April 1991 gave me joy. God blessed me with a healthy baby, free from any complications or issues. Yes, he was delivered through a caesarean section, but despite initial fears, I confronted them with strength, embracing the reality of my baby's arrival. I trusted that time would heal the wound.

After his birth, church members took turns accommodating us for different periods of time until I got temporary accommodation in a bed and breakfast named Newham Hotel. Sometimes, I looked after people's children in exchange for a roof over my head and food.

I didn't even have milk tokens for my baby. It was hard for the baby and me, especially because the baby had a good appetite. I was weak because I didn't have enough food to eat, I couldn't afford it, and my baby was dependent on milk. I struggled to breastfeed the baby, but God moved in quickly.

At a prayer meeting, I was informed by one of the attendees, Brother Mark, who was a white police officer, that any child born in the UK is entitled to milk and that all I needed to do was present my son's birth certificate to the Department for Social Security (DSS).

'I was so green,' as we say in Kenya, meaning ignorant and innocent. I didn't know the associated benefits for a child born in England. Thank God he was entitled to milk. Our lives changed from that point on. I began getting weekly milk tokens for my son. Though I did not have income support, at least the baby had food. This country was so good to me. Brother Mark was a saviour, and I can't thank him enough for helping me to feed my child.

Six months later, I introduced the baby Emmanuel to beans on toast, eggs, and tea, and he began to grow quickly.

We were housed in a bed and breakfast, and I was delighted because we had our own place and breakfast, too. This marked a significant turning point in my life. It allowed me to live with greater independence while holding onto the hope of securing more permanent housing.

I left the bed and breakfast when the local Council found me temporary accommodation in Leyton in the London borough of Waltham Forest. I remember this very well. It was no 43 Seymour Road, E10. It was a Victorian house divided into two flats; we stayed in the lower flat with two bedrooms and a garden. But we never even sat in that garden; I was so depressed and lonely that my mind was constantly churning on what to do to accomplish my dreams.

While living in Leyton, I continued attending all the church services, looking after the baby, taking him to mother and toddler groups, play schemes, and clinics for injections, visiting charity shops in Forest Gate, and seeing church friends. And I would return to our flat in the evening. My appreciation for the church remained deeply rooted in my heart. I was always fully grateful for the kindness and mercy they had shown me when I was in dire need,

At that stage, I was already transitioning, striving to establish myself. I believe the church members would have been pleased to see my determination and drive. They would likely have seen me as someone on a meaningful journey, far from reaching its end, continually moving forward and not anywhere near the end.

In Leyton, I was now on benefits and started saving my benefit, which I think was £56 weekly around 1992-93 and rose to £72.84 weekly in September 1997.

Back then, the most significant expense was my son's nappies. When I needed to buy a new packet, I just couldn't save much. But I saved all my benefits during the weeks I didn't need to. Over three years, I accumulated £4,000.

I then decided to take £3,000 of that and send £2,000 to my son's dad to get a ticket to join me and £1,000 to my sister and nephew to help them join me in the UK. It was lonely, too, without any family members, and life for them in Kenya was challenging too. I felt a strong urge to support them. I recall the days when I would take just £5 to the post office to deposit it into my instant-save Abbey National account.

How I managed to save £4,000 during some of the most challenging times of my life is still hard to comprehend, and I am struck by the realization that even during my difficult times, I found the strength to help others. During these moments, the true power of self-sacrifice and the enduring spirit of compassion kicked in.

University – different course, different country, same aim

One weekday morning in Leyton, just after breakfast, I put my baby in the pushchair to go for a stroll. We walked from our street to the main road, along Lea Bridge Road, towards an area known as Baker's Arms. It was an ordinary high street with local shops, perfect for casual high street window shopping. As I gazed through the windows of the job centre in Baker's Arms, my eyes caught sight of an advertisement for the University of North London's IT program—it read in part, 'Come and do a degree in IT in only three years. I decided to step into the job centre and inquire further. Little did I realize then that this unplanned encounter would mark the revival of my university aspirations, leading to the start of a fulfilling career journey. It's a testament to the unforeseen opportunities that can arise when we least expect them, shaping our lives in remarkable ways.

Reflecting on the demanding field of medicine, I realised that it required long hours of study over many years. With no family around to assist with the baby and limited financial resources, the prospect seemed daunting. I made the decision to switch to IT, which offered me the possibility of completing my studies and becoming independent in just three years.

I noted down the telephone number and called the University of North London, booking an appointment for an interview.

I told myself this was an excellent opportunity but was worried about where I would get the fees, even for the IT course. I wasn't entitled to a grant, yet I believed in doing something while I waited for my papers to come through. I didn't want to sit around receiving income support benefits. I had anticipated spending ten years to complete my medical school in Casablanca. For me, a degree, any degree from Great Britain, meant something. I was committed to pushing forward for any opportunity that came my way. Education was the key to my future; I'd never doubted that for a moment.

When I went to the interview at the university, it was the first time I saw a computer mouse. I didn't even know how to hold it. I remember my teacher, Mr. Michael Mumford, holding my hand, his hand on top of mine, showing me how to use the mouse.

I was offered a place at the university to pursue a BSc in Information Technology and Information Systems. I accepted, of course, without hesitation.

As I didn't qualify for a grant, I spent a lot of time in the Student Union. However, it wasn't for fun but rather to fill out forms to apply for financial grants from charity organisations.

Sometimes I got the money, but other times I didn't. I spent time researching organisations with the help of the university's Women's Officer, Paula.

Me in the library at the University of North London, circa 1992-1994

During this course of study, I usually bathed in the evening to make it easier in the morning. I would wake up early enough to prepare, dress, and feed the baby, then dress myself before heading to Plaistow tube station.

I wasn't used to this kind of life and found it hell. Every morning, I took the Overground train to North London with my two-year-old son. Looking back, I marvel at my strength and determination; I was unstoppable then, driven by the unwavering belief that I had no alternative if I wanted a better future for us. It was a necessity, not a choice, and thankfully, it paid off.

Our journey involved one stop at West Ham Station from Plaistow, where we would then catch the Overground train to Highbury and Islington. This station was both the end of our morning commute and the starting point for our journey home in the evening. For three years, my son and I used this route daily. If I was going to change our lives, I had to be committed to the cause.

I was the only student in my class who attended college with a baby. Other parents also used the creche facility as evidenced by the children I observed in there.

The Main Campus was just two minutes away from Holloway Tube Station on Holloway Road, where I spent most of my time. Still, I couldn't use this station because using the underground trains from Plaistow Station to Holloway Road meant a lot of changes: take the District Line from Plaistow down to Mile End. Change to the Central Line down to Holborn, then the Piccadilly Line to Holloway Road. That was challenging in terms of pushchairs, going up and down the stairs, and using escalators to change platforms. So, I opted to use the Overground throughout the three years because the changes between stations were not as complicated as the underground. I had come from Kisii, where there were no trains, and even the trains in Morocco were easy, so I'd never gotten used to a complex train system. This was a whole new experience for me.

After being rehoused back in Newham from Leyton, we lived in a flat in Plaistow. We journeyed every morning through the playground near the station behind these stairs below. In the year 2000, the playground benefited from me. I campaigned for improvements to that same playground for the children in the area when I led my community for the New Deal Community Initiative, which saw us being granted £54 million from the central government for the Plaistow and West Ham regeneration programmes. I continued campaigning for the area when I became a councillor in 2000.

For three years, I routinely climbed these stairs with my baby.

On most days, I carried my son in a pushchair up the stairs leading to the main road and then into Plaistow Station. When I was tired, I would push the baby along the long ramp below for pushchairs and wheelchairs, but many times, I avoided it because men used to urinate there, and I could not stand the stench.

I then crossed over to the station side before tackling further stairs down to the platform to catch a train for only one stop to West Ham, followed by the struggle of further stairs to the North London overground train platform. I rarely found somebody to help me, especially during the rush hour, so I preferred to keep moving rather than waiting for assistance, as it was also quicker for me and allowed me to make it to my lectures on time. I became quite skilled at managing this task. I struggled with the stairs by myself but was blessed with energy.

A hard struggle each day, but I was committed to completing the degree so that we didn't remain council tenants forever or dependent on income support. Britain is a country that won't leave anyone dying in a corner. They will support you and help you stand up; then, once upright, you can help yourself and give back to society. Life is about give and take. I can't complain. I remember in Morocco, during times of illness and financial strain, I resorted to using my passport as collateral in exchange for medicine at pharmacies. That would not happen in the UK, not because the pharmacy wouldn't agree to it but because I wouldn't need to resort to that. There would always be some kind of support in Britain. North Africa was only a route, or rather, a stepping stone to my destination, England. However, this route had hurdles to overcome—hunger and disease.

In the evenings, I always rushed to pick up my son while other students had the opportunity to sit, have coffee or tea, do homework together, and chat about the day. I had none of that. I rushed to the creche, picked up the baby and headed to Islington to catch the train home. If it were raining, I'd use the pushchair raincover for the baby, put the books under it, and, with my jacket on, off we went. This running up and down must have made me even stronger, like going to the river for water as a child. Sometimes, when it was raining and some trains were cancelled, it would be challenging and frustrating. Arriving home, I would prepare food, play a bit with the baby, and send him to bed as quickly as possible so that I could start my homework. There was no time to rest. When I finished one chore, there were two or more waiting. But I always managed to get everything done, which is why I say these were indeed blessed struggles.

It was different to the struggles to gain an education back at home. I had arduous journeys and endless household chores waiting for me when I got home. Then, when all such domestic duties were finally complete, I had to open my book and start studying. There's no other way if education is to be the route out of poverty. At least I had access to electric light, modern heating systems, and running water within the confines of my house, but I was lonely and had long hours of work.

I applied to the hardship fund and was awarded funding for my own desktop computer from charitable organisations. One time, this computer was not working, and I reached out to the university's help desk for assistance, but they asked me to bring it in; I was stuck, as it would be really difficult to take my child and the desktop all the way across London.

Fortunately, a stroke of luck came my way when Craig, a fellow student from my group who had a vehicle, offered to help. He kindly drove to my house, and we transported the broken laptop to the university's help desk for repair. This experience highlighted the importance of both support systems and the spirit of camaraderie within the university community.

The memory of a fellow student willingly coming to my home to transport my laptop to the student help desk still astonishes me. Reflecting on that moment, it's incredible to think about the level of understanding and kindness that existed among people back then. This student wasn't even a romantic partner; he was simply a study group member. Despite living on the other side of London, he generously volunteered to drive to East London, pick up my laptop, and take it to the college help desk for me. Moreover, he would return it to my house once the task was completed.

I can't help but feel incredibly blessed to have encountered such compassionate individuals during my university journey. Their willingness to help without any personal gain is genuinely remarkable, and I hold an immense appreciation for their kindness. The memory of Craig's selflessness and the support I received from him and others like him remains a source of gratitude and inspiration.

One instance is when I had to apply for a hardship fund to purchase two textbooks. The first book was 'Business Process Engineering,' priced at £20, and the other 'Advanced Relational Databases' costing around £18. Receiving the grant brought me immense joy, as I could finally own these essential resources and study at my own pace from home. The convenience of having my own books and computer allowed me to work comfortably without needing to stay at the college for reading or research.

Another memorable aspect of university life was participating in study groups with my friends. Before heading home, we would gather to discuss, write notes, and then continue elaborating on the topics at home.

One cherished memory was during lunch breaks. A friend from South Africa and I used to visit a Turkish cafe. We indulged in chips and saveloy, a delectable treat. Our routine involved adding mayonnaise and ketchup for extra flavour. We were on a tight budget, so we requested tap water instead of a soft drink. Despite our modest choices, those moments were enjoyable and strengthened our special bond.

These experiences at university, from obtaining the grant for textbooks to forming study groups and enjoying simple yet satisfying meals, added a unique charm to my academic journey.

During my time at university, I recall another time vividly illustrating our financial constraints. My friend from South Africa, another friend from Ghana, and I would occasionally treat ourselves to a visit to a nearby Chinese restaurant close to the university. The highlight of these visits was the Chinese fried rice, which was simply exquisite. To this day, I've searched high and low for a rice dish that could rival the one from that restaurant, but I've never found one.

In a state of financial limitation, this experience took on a unique dimension. With limited funds, a single portion of the Chinese fried rice would vanish almost instantly as soon as I took a bite. The satisfaction it brought was unlike any other, leaving me yearning for more. However, my friend from Ghana had a different experience. Her financial circumstances were more comfortable, thanks to her parents being in Britain and her father's Italian background. This allowed her the luxury of indulging in the restaurant without the same constraints.

These experiences were a part of what I consider the challenging times in the UK. During those moments, I lacked the necessary support and financial security to rely on.

I remember hosting a party at my house and inviting my friends from college. They all showed up, and we had a fantastic time together. It was a true house party experience, though not extravagant by any means. Our party essentials included bottles of Coke, some rice, and drumsticks. Despite the simplicity, it was a wonderful gathering filled with fun and camaraderie. Unfortunately, I have lost contact with most of my university classmates.

The memory of those sausages, saveloys, and chips I had during my university days still astonishes me. The food was so incredibly enjoyable. I believe it's partly due to the physical demands of studying, the lack of money, and limited food resources. This combination seemed to make even the simplest meals taste exceptional.

Food, or rather the hunger I experienced during those times, has been a constant presence in my life. I am deeply grateful that I have enough to eat now. Whenever I reflect on my university days and early life, memories of hunger resurface. It's as if those memories trigger an immediate desire to eat something. The strong connection between those experiences and my yearning for food is undeniable.

Revisiting The Daily Journey

In 2020, I returned to the University of North London to revisit the route I used to take with my son when he was a baby. I started from the stairs in Plaistow, which was my first challenge every morning before the stations. And what do I come across?

I revisited Spring House, the site of the University Nursery/creche where I dropped off my son every morning for three years, for the first time since 1995. I aimed to document this experience for my children and my readers, hoping to motivate and inspire others who aspire to overcome the barriers we encounter in life by going the extra mile.

As I documented my journey to the University in 2020, I encountered a man urinating, the same way I used to find 28 years ago.

On days when I had lectures at 9:30, I had to rush to drop off my son to make it to class on time. I would rush out to catch a bus three stops down the street to the Holloway Road Building for lectures. The good thing is that my son wasn't a crybaby, and he enjoyed the crèche a lot, which gave me peace of mind. As soon as I dropped him off, he would run off to his friends.

In 2020 - Spring House, which was almost opposite the station. This is where the creche was and where I left my son most days before going on to the other sites of the university for my lectures. I would pick him up in the evening for the return journey. I used to have only one lecture a week in this building, but I could go at lunch time and peep through the window and see him. He was happy with the other children, and off I went to the main building,

In April 1995 - Spring House creche.
My son is the one next to the male carer.

In the creche- my son blowing his four candles on his birthday
in April 1995.

My 2020 visit when I went to document my route to the University of North London- I used to spend so much time at the Student Union that it felt like I had my own office there when I was dedicated to seeking assistance from hardship funds and completing various application forms.

My 2020 visit - My dream came true here with my first degree, a BSc Hons 2:2 in Information Systems and Technology.

A lot of improvements have been made over the last thirty years. Nothing stands still, and nothing should.

Opposite this block was the Computer Science and IT Building, where I spent most of my time, but it seems that the building has been sold to a business. Why not if it helps fund the university and allows investment for the future? On the other side were Maida Vale, Ladbroke House, and Spring House, where I used to leave my son daily.

I spent some time in Highbury, Islington, and the Main Campus near Holloway Road Station. I remember that only desktop publishing was taught in Ladbroke House. When I had lectures near Holloway, it was easy, but when they were at Maida Vale and Ladbroke, I'd be running like mad after the lectures to catch up with crèche time.

After three years, I finished my Information Systems and Information Technology course, qualifying for and graduating with a Bachelor of Science degree. I got the university education I had dreamed of back home throughout my childhood.

I was on my journey, passing a significant milestone and one that would branch off to considerable opportunities.

Another Round of Education

I was committed to education and wanted to go all the way. Education became the chassis of the vehicle I took on my journey. In 1995, I went to Barclays Bank, took out a Career

Development Loan and embarked on a postgraduate degree in Information Technology and Knowledge Engineering, emphasising knowledge elicitation processes, at Middlesex University. I was offered a place on the programme in Bounds Green, Northwest London.

The world of medicine was now indeed in the past, and my new and consuming passion was Information Communications and Technology, better known by the acronym ICT. This second degree was different from the hectic and tension-filled journeys up and down from one tube station to another with my son in his pushchair.

Now, I was the only woman in a class of nine. A smaller class meant closer interaction with the lecturers, fewer lessons, and more consultation between students and lecturers and among the learners. My project and dissertation were on knowledge elicitation. My second degree from an English university was different but, in many ways, just as much a struggle as the first, my son being six years old and needing my full attention.

Middlesex was further away, taking me an hour by train, and so the rush to get to college and return to my son was still in evidence and almost as intense as in my undergraduate days.

We had one class party at the end of the year, but it was something small just to bring us together and bid each other goodbye. During the course, there had been no time for me to party. The boys had more fun as they went out together each Friday. One of them had a car so they could all get in and go as I rushed home to be with my son.

I had the motivation, mainly because I knew where I came from. Life at home in Kenya was tough, and I knew that if I went back there with not one but two degrees, my life would be so much better. Kenya respects degrees from the UK, and therefore, getting a job would be easier.

Then, I told myself that now that I had crossed that bridge of education, it was time for me to settle down. What next? What I didn't realize was that the more qualifications I gained, the more I wanted to read further. I was bitten by the bug for learning. What was going on? Then, I remembered a phrase from home that seemed to fit perfectly:

'Songa mbele,' (move forward and keep going)

I told myself this many times. This is a girl who was always thirsty for education, for knowledge, and to learn. I had dreamed of getting an education but had never been sure it would become a reality.

'Endelea' (go on)

I cheered myself on. My priority became getting more qualifications so that I could use my knowledge on any platform I came across at work. I became addicted to my studies. I remember when, at my first job, I was still studying for professional qualifications. I went on to become a Microsoft Certified Technology Specialist.

I think what drove me was the extreme difficulty in getting an education back home in Kenya. In July 1997, I was awarded a Master of Science degree in Information Technology and Knowledge Engineering from Middlesex University.

Endelea, songa mbele (Continue, move forward)

My health and that of my son blossomed like lilies of the valley. In 1999, as I traveled back to Kenya with my son Emmanuel, I was laden with a wealth of qualifications and confidence. On that airplane, I felt assured, proud, and confident, carrying with me a treasure trove of accomplishments to share with my family and Emmanuel's father: a handsome son, numerous qualifications, and the privilege of British citizenship.

Revisiting Middlesex university after 23 years

I went back to Middlesex University, where I pursued my Masters, and was struck by the changes that had occurred. Some of the buildings had been transformed into flats, and I couldn't even recognise the places I used to frequent. The experience was rather sad. I wish I had captured photographs during my time there.

Even the train station, where I used to disembark, had changed. Returning after three decades, it was astonishing to witness how much the memory of places can fade when they've undergone such transformations. I wish I had at least taken pictures of the chip shop and Chinese restaurant in North London.

My advice to you is that if you've had significant experiences at any institution, document them through photos. This can help preserve memories, especially if changes occur over time.

CHAPTER THIRTEEN
WORK AFTER GRADUATION

After completing my master's degree in 1997, I enthusiastically ventured into the world of work. I secured my first job, which lasted for only two weeks, at the Royal London Hospital as an IT trainer. I taught MS Office Applications to doctors and nurses. However, the reality of the workplace stood in stark contrast to the academic realm. My initial enthusiasm wavered as panic set in upon realising my lack of basic work skills, like sending emails. The gap between university and professional life was bigger than I had anticipated. The challenge of being a single-parent immigrant with no family support, constantly struggling to make ends meet, made the first job experience even more daunting.

Driven by my anxieties, coupled with what I perceived as a lack of support from my boss, I hastily left the job without following proper protocols. I didn't contact the employment agency or seek any guidance. This abrupt decision led to me having to return the payment I had received for Christmas, as requested by the NHS. My actions were impulsive and a reflection of my uncertainty and lack of experience.

I realised the importance of grasping email etiquette, workplace communication, and the intricacies of daily operations. This experience underscored the value of coupling academic knowledge with practical skills. I emerged from this lesson with newfound wisdom. I now understand the significance of addressing such gaps early on. For instance, the simple act of seeking help, like requesting a handover, could have alleviated my challenges during those initial days on the job.

By the year 2000, I had found my footing as an IT engineer at the City of Westminster College, a position I held for a fulfilling five years. I regard this as the first proper job of my career, which I started there at the age of 38.

For some, beginning a career at 38 might be daunting, but I never allowed age to define my path. I didn't feel the need to conform to societal expectations of home ownership or starting a family. During that period, my focus was to get a job and truly start living after we had been just surviving for a long time. I was at peace, brimming with energy and had little concern for maintaining a healthy routine, diet, or exercise regimen. It was a time free from such worries, and to be honest, I was healthy. I welcomed my second child at 40 and left this job when I was 43 years old. These events marked significant milestones in my journey, reminding me that life doesn't always follow conventional timelines.

To boost my confidence as an IT Engineer, I pursued a Microsoft Certified Professional (MSP) qualification. I embarked on the journey, securing valuable certifications. This marked the inception of my professional voyage. I continued to pursue additional Microsoft qualifications to cement my expertise.

I realised I could not depend solely on a company to advance my career. Waiting for conventional company appraisals and promotions meant that my progress depended on the company's decisions. I decided to take control of my career by focusing on self-improvement and qualifications. This approach allowed me to plan and advance my career more rapidly, and the results were ultimately rewarding.

I went on to become a Microsoft-certified professional technology specialist, which greatly boosted my confidence as an IT engineer.

Collaboration was the bedrock of this role; within it, I felt a surge of achievement and personal growth. It was after five years in this job that I unearthed my potential and discovered my affinity for project management.

I yearned for a job where I could sit comfortably in a suit rather than donning a t-shirt while crawling under desks to fix cables or working in server rooms and setting up computers. While I had become proficient in tasks ranging from configuring profiles to managing firewalls, I knew it was time for a change. This led me to embark on another journey into project management, a decision I have never regretted.

Moving into project management, I used my strong IT background to my advantage. The combination of my IT education and growing skills in project management gave me new confidence and energy. At first, it was tough but immensely rewarding.

Alongside the IT-focused qualifications, I took around a dozen more qualifications to enhance my skills and knowledge of project management. These included PRINCE2 (Projects in Controlled Environments) Foundation and Practitioner levels, Managing Successful Programmes, Management of Risk, and the planning and support tools SharePoint, Primavera P6 and Project Server. I then started looking for jobs in project management and found that I was really good at them. This led to work opportunities in different European countries, including big projects in the UK, Germany, Sweden, and briefly, the Netherlands. I wouldn't have traveled to these countries without my qualifications. My qualifications were like a passport, opening doors to opportunities and experiences I never thought were possible.

My journey took place in diverse sectors in the UK, encompassing periods at banks like Lloyds TSB, Barclay's, RBS, and Nationwide. I was stationed at Stokely Park as a planner for British Petroleum in 2007, providing project support to ensure the smooth delivery of projects.

I also enjoyed working with the Department for Work and Pensions, which took me across diverse locations such as Newcastle and Blackpool. As a planner, I cherished this role as well. The experience allowed me to explore picturesque places like Newcastle, with a beautiful journey from London through

Durham and York. During my time there, I had the chance to visit Lord Collingwood's monument and Mosley Street in Newcastle. Mosley Street is historically the first public street to be illuminated with electricity, thanks to Joseph Swan, who hailed from Sunderland and invented the first lightbulb. I truly relished this role, stationed at Cobalt Business Centre in Newcastle, which is also the biggest business park in the north of England.

Subsequently, I transitioned to the government sector, where my freelance roles led me to the Ministry of Justice, the Department for Environmental Agency, the Rural Payments Agency (RPA), the Home Office, the Metropolitan Police Service, the Royal Mail and Post Office separation programme as well as Transport for London and a Southwest Rail upgrade programme and also the DLR (Dockland Light Railway Metro in London). Immersion in these roles provided rich interactions with civil servants and a valuable contribution to significant national rollout programs. Using my planning skills, I meticulously crafted project plans, thereby orchestrating the successful execution of these programs. My knack for balancing risks, milestones, dependencies, and reporting became my strength. I enjoyed mentoring junior project support staff and sharing my knowledge and experience in the details of project and programme delivery.

One of my contracts was based in Swindon. Fatigue from my work once led me to fall asleep on the train home, and by the time I woke up, I was on a return journey back to Swindon. This is a reminder of the long hours and early mornings I dedicated to my professional pursuits.

These diverse experiences primed me for my next chapter, working in Europe, where I anticipated further expanding my horizons.

Work in UK and Europe

Before embarking on my European journey, I took on a pivotal role that significantly shaped my path – I became a Councillor for the Borough Council of Newham. This experience, which you'll find detailed later, added a new dimension to my life's narrative. I transitioned into a new phase of project management roles across Europe. This shift marked a turning point in my career. I distinctly remember my debut assignment in Sweden, where I joined Volvo Cars in Gothenburg as a project planner. The opportunity to work in a foreign country, engage with new colleagues, and immerse myself in a different work culture was genuinely exhilarating.

My subsequent European assignments led me to Germany, where I first worked for the Ministry of Defense (British Forces Germany) at Monchengladbach, then with Bombardier in Berlin. I then took another role in Sweden, this time for the ABB Railway Electronic Upgrade Programme of the largest train company in Sweden.

Working in Germany, I had the privilege to visit different cities, which were both rewarding and challenging experiences. In Poland, I explored the cities of Szczecin and Sulubis, and in Germany, I had the chance to discover Dusseldorf and Cologne, with their impressive cathedrals. Additionally, I visited the Holocaust Memorial, a poignant reminder of history's significance. And I remember when I saw the Cologne Cathedral saying, 'God, I am not worthy to be here, but ye say so, and I am here.' As a youngster, I had never dreamt of working in Germany, as a black girl from Kisii in rural Africa.

Life has a way of leading us to achieve our dreams, sometimes when we least expect it. My short trip to Poland from Germany started as a simple visit out of curiosity, to explore the neighboring country. Later, as I began writing my book, I realized this visit led me to the country that I was originally supposed to study in through my scholarship.

However, my German journey also included an unfortunate incident. One morning, while having breakfast at the Holiday Inn in Monchengladbach, I briefly left my bag under a table to fetch my meal from a breakfast buffet. When I came back, I found that my bag was gone. It had important things like my Passport, iPhone, iPod, memory sticks, and portable hard disk, plus some money and makeup. Losing this bag upset me a lot because it had sentimental value; it was no longer in production, and the original one held special memories, like carrying it at my daughter's baptism. It was the first expensive handbag I had ever bought a £575 Mulberry. The effort to find a replacement on eBay was an attempt to regain what was lost, but the emotional loss remained.

Despite this setback, my subsequent trip to Germany for my second role in 2014, working with Bombardier in Berlin, was much more positive. This time, I made a conscious effort to safeguard my belongings. Additionally, my tenure in Holland allowed me to seize the opportunity to visit The Hague, home to the Supreme Court and a hub for human rights cases. This visit provided valuable insights into the significance of The Hague as a symbol of international justice.

Through all my experiences, good and challenging, living in Germany and traveling across Europe has made me understand different cultures, people, and history better. Each new experience has helped me grow both professionally and personally.

I also had the chance to work in the Netherlands for a short time, where I contributed to Calvin Klein in Rotterdam and ING Bank in Amsterdam.

Working as a freelancer in Sweden was a refreshing experience. I had the opportunity to collaborate with Swedish professionals, learn about their work culture, and contribute to projects in a foreign setting. All of which was really rewarding. Interacting with colleagues in Gothenburg, a city known for its innovation and vibrant atmosphere, introduced me to new insights and perspectives.

Getting used to the different ways of working, the language, and daily life in Sweden helped me understand more about working with people from around the world.

This experience not only expanded my professional skill set but also allowed me to form meaningful connections with people from different walks of life. I was reminded once again of the adaptability and resilience that are crucial in the ever-changing global work environment. The lessons learned during my time in Sweden continue to shape my approach to cross-cultural teamwork and effective project management.

I remember a touching moment clearly. A colleague showed us Hällsnäs, one of the tallest rocks in the city and a famous landmark. During a quiet moment, they mentioned that, sadly, this beautiful place is known for being a spot where some people have chosen to end their lives. This experience made me think deeply about how complex and delicate life can be, even in the most beautiful places.

Working in Europe added a lot to my professional and personal life. Trying the local foods in Germany, Sweden, and the Netherlands was fun. For example, the Bavarian dish in Germany with its different sausages was perfect for anyone who loves meat. In Sweden, people focus on eating healthily and staying active with things like jogging, which I found interesting. It's amazing how working in a new place can also lead you to explore and enjoy its culture.

My education and skills have made me who I am today and have given me experience from around the world. As a Kenyan-British woman, I am a proud ready and willing to put my expertise and experience to work for the benefit of both Kenya and the UK.

Sometimes, I ask myself how I stayed focused. It's one thing when you're young and desperate for change, as I was in Kenya and even in Morocco. However, the struggle through the streets and stations of East and North London, humping around with my son's pushchair and rushing everywhere for the next class or to pick up my son from creche for home time, was another level of struggle altogether. The answer to the question of staying focused was that I now had someone depending on me, my little boy.

My boy was precisely the point. It came to a stage when I told myself that if I had another baby without ways of supporting it, the suffering for all of us would be forever. Then, I focused on becoming a game changer. It would have made sense for me to look for work after my first degree and start earning money then. I wasn't so young, but I had incredible energy, and I believed that the higher I climbed in terms of qualifications, the greater my earnings would be. With a keen awareness of the limited time available to achieve my goals, I aimed higher and higher to accomplish as much as possible. I knew that there would be light at the end of it all. Whether in Kenya or the UK, because, after all my qualifications, I was putting myself on the world stage, not just in the UK or Kenya.

But I also think much of it was because my background was a difficult one. And I believe so much that if you try and work hard, you will surely see good results. Good things and success in life are brought about by working hard and not listening to negative people, nor self-pity about being a single mum and not British. Blame games were not for me. I knew that these would push me backwards and not forward to take advantage of all the opportunities that came along, plus the risks. I even told myself that I would study so that by the time I'm kicked out of the UK, I will have acquired the necessary qualifications to be internationally recognised. It was clear that there were more opportunities in England than in Kenya and Morocco for me. So, my intention was simply to seize those opportunities. Little did I know that this was working in my favour and that God had destined the UK to become my home. By the time the paper to remain in Britain was legalised, I was already a professional in IT with Microsoft and teaching at the Pitman Training Centre in Romford as a technology specialist.

Around the same time my paperwork with the Home Office was getting sorted out, I had just finished my master's degree and become a Microsoft Certified Professional. At the same time, I started working as a People's Representative in the London Borough of Newham, where I served as a councillor for an amazing ten years. It was quite a coincidence how everything fell into place so well. Life was working out perfectly, and I never would have thought this path would make me a proud British citizen.

One consideration to note is that I was supporting myself at this stage and no longer on state benefits. I've never returned to state benefits, something I'm happy and proud about.

I also believe that God, like His creations, doesn't like lazy people. Employers don't want lazy workers, and even parents tell their children to be hard-working. If we do our part, God will finish the job for us. If everyone tries their best in whatever they're doing, the world would be a much better place.

While this achievement may not look big, it was a significant milestone in my life, considering my background. I never dreamt of being a politician in London, and here I was, representing a ward, listening to their issues, and advising and seeking solutions for them from the council. The parallels with my mum becoming a community leader are there to see; Mum finally found her way, as I did.

A good grounding in the word of God is key to my success. Naming my son Emmanuel, meaning 'God is with us,' was forever encouraging.

Project Management

Studying in the UK presented me with many opportunities. It enabled me to work in various fields and industries, first as an IT specialist and then as a planner. Some big names include ABB, Southwest Railways (SWR), Transport for London (TFL), the Metropolitan Police (MPS), Balfour Beatty, the Environmental Agency, Banks like Lloyds, Barclays, Royal Bank of Scotland (RBS), and Nationwide, Calvin Klein, Volvo, Bombardier, the Ministry of Justice, Royal Mail, BP, Home Office UK, and the Ministry of Defense, based in Germany.

Looking back, I'm amazed at how far I've come from my simple beginnings: carrying water and firewood over a wobbly bridge, going hungry and feeling scared, dealing with the taboo of circumcision, and dealing with rats that bit my mom's heels and safari ants that attacked us while we slept on the ground. Our house had holes in the roof - we saw stars at night, rain came in through the same holes. I have come from living with no proper windows, doors or electricity, or running water, and sleeping on the floor with inadequate blankets, to becoming a landlord in the bustling city of London. My childhood was tough, with bullies taunting and threatening me back in Kenya near the river. But I kept moving forward quietly and with determination. Every time I fell, I got back up and continued, knowing that perseverance would guide me forward. My experience has taught me one thing: that no matter how difficult the circumstances may seem, there is always hope for a brighter future. Keep trying until you get it.

Education has been a key part of my journey. Even though it took a long time to get my qualifications, I never let my age stop me. I followed my dream of education to become qualified to work anywhere in the world, whether it be Kenya, Morocco, or the UK.

CHAPTER FOURTEEN

FOR TEN YEARS AN ELECTED REPRESENTATIVE

At the start of the new millennium, I entered the corridors of power in Britain, mixing with many of the great political figures of the day. The photos explain this better than I can explain in words. I was on holiday in Kenya in 2000 when an event that would change my life dramatically happened in my local ward in the London Borough of Newham. My councillor, Harbans Jabbal, died, a by-election was called, and party nominations were held and closed. I didn't find out about any of this until I returned to my home in Plaistow, East London. I took one look at the names of the nominees and detected what I regarded as a serious anomaly. None of the candidates were from my ward. I expressed the fear that this would disenfranchise the constituents because nominees who did not hail from our ward could claim to know our challenges. I demanded that the nominations be reopened so that I could enter the race. As luck would have it, this happened, and I became a candidate.

Truth be told, I had never at any one time, even fleetingly, thought of myself as a politician, much less running to be an elected representative. Popular reputation has it that my mother was effective as a clan elder and used to represent our village's chief. She would relay local issues to the chief and the chief's edicts to the community. The chief would rely on her to solve problems arising in the community. I have also been told that my family can trace its lineage to that of Senior Chief Zachariah Angwenyi, regarded by many as the patriarch of Abagetutu, and former Kitutu Chache MP Jimmy Angwenyi, all of whom are descended from my great great grandfathers. But while I knew I could lead; I never thought it would be as a political representative.

Nevertheless, I had thrown my hat in the ring, and there was no looking back. It was easy for me to pick Labour as my party of choice. It was the party my neighbours, fellow immigrants, student colleagues, and the struggling majority in my ward identified with. It was a progressive party.

I campaigned as a resident of the ward whose children went to school in the ward and who, therefore, understood the challenges facing the ward and its communities. Being a single mom who worked hard to graduate from university with my child in a pushchair, having two degrees, working various jobs, and being deeply passionate about education — these experiences made my campaign strong. I was already a governor at three schools and argued that it was important for someone like me to run because our community needed a voice. I pointed out that many of our young people were unemployed. We needed ideas that would lead to a generation of jobs to enable our people to put money in their pockets and make life liveable. I argued for improved childcare facilities for children up to five years of age. I knew the availability of these centres would make a massive difference to the lives of single mums struggling to earn a living, attend college and better their lives.

I pointed to the neglected alleyways that acted as dens of crime for teenagers. I asked for support from teachers and called for the improvement of council houses, from which many children woke up to go to school. I addressed the challenges of youth and made a strong pitch for education as a way of changing lives. And, given my background, I would have been remiss if I had not taken on matters of minority groups, especially those struggling with English, which often leads to discrimination. In the minds of some of my supporters, I did not have to run because I had a good education and job. But I was driven by a mission to help marginalised communities.

When the results were in, I had won Plaistow North for Labour, garnering 826 votes to the Conservative runner-up's 585. According to The Newham Recorder, a local paper, the turnout was 21.14 per cent, 'which is high for a by-election in Newham and included a record 140 postal and proxy voters.' I was now an elected representative of the people. As their councillor, I was the Deputy Chair of the Corporate Scrutiny Committee, a lead member of the Domestic Violence Against Women, and a member of the 2012 Olympic Park

Committee, which was massive because it involved decanting people from Olympic sites and also because I had to canvass for our people to get jobs on the Olympic sites. I held my weekly advice surgery in Stratford, where my constituents came in to raise and discuss issues affecting them that needed my attention.

Here is a pictorial presentation of my decade of life as a London politician:

With Hilary Armstrong, the Minister for Local Government, at the 1998 Labour Party Conference in Brighton, where I represented my community. We believed in a good life for all. Our joy can be seen in our relaxed arms. It was announced that £54 million would be granted for the regeneration of the New Deal for Communities (NDC) area in Plaistow and West Ham. This was after tireless work that included many meetings and walkabouts to identify issues and collect evidence to enable us to make our case to the central government.

The NDC funded capital projects, including knocking down tower blocks and building new homes, improving schools, reducing crime, and creating resource centres for the youth.

Board Members of the New Deal for Communities, with Junior Minster and MP Beverley Hughes next to me during her Plaistow and West Ham visit and walkabout in 2000. John Thorne, second from the left, was a fellow councillor.

With visiting Minister for Communities Beverley Hughes in 1998 when I was a community leader. An awesome picture of two beautiful ladies. I was on course to improve the lives of ordinary people in the community, and we made it after that 10-year initiative.

Candidates line up in poll battle

VOTERS in Plashet Ward have a date with the polling stations on February 24 to fill the Town Hall vacancy caused by the death of Harban Jabbal.

The by-election was confirmed when a total of three candidates were officially registered for the poll battle.

Labour are looking to Regina Williams to retain the seat while the Conservatives have put their faith in Reza Ahmed Shafi Choudhury.

The Newham Independents Association have Mr Swaminathan Bazlakrishnan, who is commonly known as Dr Bala, in their corner.

Mr Jabbal, a father of six, died on December 31 last year in Newham General Hospital from a lung infection. He was elected in May, 1998.

The build-up in the Newham Recorder of February 2, 2000.

PLASHET WARD BY-ELECTION Thursday 24 FEBRUARY 2000

There is a by-election in Plashet ward on Thursday 24 February 2000.

The **Labour Party** candidate is Regina Williams. **Regina** knows Plashet ward very well:

Regina Williams, Labour Party candidate, with Tony Banks MP

- Regina lives in Plashet ward and her son goes to school in the ward
- Regina is a community leader representing the Plaistow North area in the New Deal for Communities. Working with other local people, she has helped to win £55million from the Government. A lot of this money is to spent in the Brooks Road estate and surrounding roads on improving housing, health, education and the environment, and tackling crime
- Regina has been a Governor at Portway school.

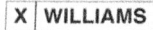

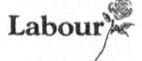

Published by J Thorne, 84 East Rd. E15.
Printed by Allen Cramp & Co Ltd. 50 Holness Rd. E15.

The start of the journey. Campaigning with local MP Tony Banks.

Plashet ward

Since May 1998, the date of the last local elections, Newham Council and your local councillor John Thorne, have worked with local people to:

- introduce CCTV in Green St
- start on improvements to Queens Market and in Green St, which include better and wider pavements, festive lighting and a more welcoming Queens Market
- continue to improve many pavements in the ward and give homeowners a contribution to improve front garden walls
- get empty garages demolished at the back of the flats in Fothergill Close
- spend money from Europe on training and employment initiatives in the ward.

X	WILLIAMS

New Deal for Communities

Local people and Newham Council have recently won £55million to spend around Plaistow and West Ham stations. This includes properties to the north and south of Stratford Rd, up to West Rd. Money is to be spent on:

- better facilities at Portway school: local teacher assistants in all infant classes, more IT, initiatives to keep high quality staff
- tackling crime, eg. in Lettsom Walk and other walkways
- improving the quality of housing, especially of council-owned property
- increasing employment opportunities by providing childcare, makerting job opportunities and targeted support for unemployed people
- initiatives to promote better health.

Published by J Thorne, 84 East Rd, E15
Printed by Allen Cramp & Co Ltd, 50 Holness Rd, E15

Regina Williams

Regina Williams is the Labour party candidate in the Plashet by-election on Thursday 24 February.

Regina knows Plashet ward very well:
- Regina lives in Plashet ward
- Regina is a community leader who helped to win £55million for New Deal for Communities
- Regina has been a Governor of Portway school.

My 2000 campaign leaflet telling constituents
why they should vote for me.

The build-up in the Newham Recorder
of February 2, 2000.

New Councillor elected for Plashet

Regina Williams is the new councillor for the Plashet Ward. She held the seat for Labour in the February 24 by-election which followed the sudden death of Councillor Harbans Singh Jabbal.

Votes cast were: Regina Williams (Labour) 826, Reza Ahmed Shafi Choudbury (Conservative) 585, Swaminathan Balakrishnan (Newham Independest Association) 135. There was a 21.14% turnout.

How the Newham Recorder reported my 2000 victory

Presenting trophies at a local carnival in Plaistow during my first term in 2001. Events such as this bring people together and strengthen the sense of community.

Regina Williams has been a Councillor in the Plaistow area, and lives in the ward. Regina was involved in the successful New Deal for Communities bid which gained £54 million for the local area. She is a governor at Lister and Northern Road Schools. Regina's main interests on the council are developing employment opportunities, and ensuring the involvement of local residents in decision-making.

For more information, to vote by post, or to join the Labour Party call
020 8534 5040

My 2002 campaign leaflet highlights my credentials.

I secured my second poll win for the 2002-2006 term.

In for the third term from 2006 to 2010, this time representing Stratford and New Town, which included the home of the 2012 London Olympics.

4   18th April 2007

Reach out and learn about Eastern European culture

RESIDENTS are invited to celebrate Newham's Eastern European communities at a free event hosted by Stratford and West Ham Community Forum.

Reaching out to Communities will be held on next Saturday, between 12pm and 5pm at the Old Town Hall, Stratford.

Community Lead Councillor for Stratford and West Ham Regina Williams said: "This event is the per-

fect chance for people of all backgrounds to get to know each other and to learn more about one of the borough's newest communities."

Participants will be able to experience cultural entertainment with music and dance from Albanian, Lithuanian, Polish, Romanian, Roma Gypsy and Russian groups. Those keen to learn some steps can take part in a workshop on Balkan Dance moves.

As captured in this 2007 article, I pursued an inclusive agenda and reached out to all communities at every opportunity.

I welcomed Prime Minister Gordon Brown to Newham Town Hall in June 2009 and took him around to greet local people. There was a big crowd cheering him. It was beautiful and a once-in-a-lifetime opportunity for me. I shook hands with the Prime Minister. I had never dreamed of such a thing, but it happened. This, to me, was big time. Primetime coverage on Sky News TV and in the local and national newspapers gave me confidence and self-belief. MP Harriet Harman (extreme left) served in several cabinet and shadow cabinet positions during the premierships of Tony Blair and Brown. Behind me is my ward councillor colleague, Richard Crawford.

With MP Dianne Abbott and the late local MP Tony Banks, who was later elevated to the House of Lords as Lord Stratford. Abbott rose to become Shadow Home Secretary (2016 to 2020) under the leadership of Labour Party leader Jeremy Corbyn.

Abbott and Banks helped raise my profile for the campaign of 2000.

Shaking hands with David Blunkett in the House of Commons filled me with happiness. Blunkett was Blair's Home Secretary. He was a sweet man.

With Tony Banks and Tessa Jowell. Jowell, also since deceased, who served as Secretary of State for Digital, Culture, Media and Sport and Minister for the Cabinet Office between 2001-2007. I visited the House of Commons soon after it was announced that Stratford, where I had been a councillor from 2006 to 2010, would host the 2012 London Olympics.

With Chelsea fans, Tony and my son Emmanuel. Tony loved my son Emmanuel to bits. Both were Chelsea supporters, and their April birthdays were only a day apart. Tony was a gift to my family, and I miss him.

Tony Banks, our close friend and MP, invited us for a meal in the House of Commons. His widow Sally is on the right of the picture. They were a sweet couple.

The Express   www.stratfordandnewhamexpre

Domestic violence: Help break the cycle

By EXPRESS REPORTER

● Cllr Regina Williams - 'It's a voluntary programme where people can change if they want to'

NEWHAM Council is strengthing its battle against domestic violence.

It has joined up with an intervention charity to support survivors of domestic violence and keep women and children safe by educating abusers.

Currently there are 23 men who are taking part in the Domestic Violence Intervention Project, which also includes Barking and Dagenham and Waltham Forest councils, most of whom have been referred by social services.

Newham Councillor Regina Williams, who has a special brief to help reduce domestic violence, said: "This is a voluntary programme where people who want to change their behaviour towards a spouse or partner can break the cycle of domestic violence."

Perpetrators are assessed and if they are suitable begin a 32-week programme, designed to help them understand how their behaviour affects their victim. It also teaches them to be aware of their anger, to recognise the signs that build up to violence and how they can manage their temper.

Programme manager Phil Price, based in Romford Road, Stratford, said: "Our main objective in providing a programme for men to address their behaviour is to help make women and children safer.

"Perpetrators are given an opportunity to end behaviour that is destructive to them, their partners and their children.

"If they want to change, we can teach them how."

Cllr Williams added: "This is not a soft option, nor is it an alternative to court.

"We will continue to prosecute anyone who abuses their partner whilst offering the appropriate help and support to victims of domestic violence."

The new scheme is part of the Newham Council's overall strategy to reduce domestic violence. It is part of other early intervention schemes to keep victims of domestic violence safe from abusive partners or ex-partners.

One such example is the Sanctuary Scheme that provides security measures for victims who want to live in their own home. It is run in partnership with the Police.

Victims of domestic violence can ring the following numbers for help and advice:

East London Domestic Violence Intervention Project
0208 555 897
Newham Council's Domestic Violence and Hate Crime Unit
020 8430 2000 x22793
Sanctuary Scheme
020 8430 6499
Police Community Safety Unit
020 7275 5707
Lesbian, Gay, Bisexual, Transexual Helpline
08000 327 291

More achievements and moving in the right direction theme as reported by the Stratford and Newham Express of April 18, 2007.

atfordandnewhamexpress.co.uk   **The Express**

Award win for fighting abuse and violence

NEWHAM council has won an award for its campaign to challenge domestic violence.

The gong was presented by Mayor of London Ken Livingstone at City Hall on Monday.

A new child protection officer has also started work to tackle the taboos of child cruelty in Newham.

Domestic violence includes physical, sexual, emotional, psychological and financial abuse.

It accounts for about one-quarter of violent crime and victims may be men, women, children or vulnerable adults.

Newham Council's campaign included posters on buses using the vows

By CHARLOTTE SMITH

'love, honour and obey', 'till death do us part' and 'for better, for worse'. Information announcements were made over the tannoy at Stratford train station.

Purple rubber wrist bands with the telephone number for Newham Domestic Violence Forum were also given out.

The council was congratulated for its good practice and innovation in 'challenging social tolerance' at the fifth annual London awards.

The recognition came just after the United Nations International Day for the Elimination of Violence Against Women.

White ribbons and rubber wrist bands were given out in Stratford shopping centre on Thursday.

The council also raised £85 for a women's refuge and distributed information leaflets.

Head of the domestic violence and hate crime service Frances Martineau said: "We are committed to making sure Newham is a safe place for domestic violence survivors to live and we will take action against its perpetrators."

A specialist social worker will also tackle child cruelty including witchcraft, honour violence, trafficking and female genital mutilation.

Zainab Adan has a brief to work with community and faith groups to improve their understanding of child protection issues.

Zainab, 28, said: "There is a big hurdle of secrecy and shame which keeps certain traditions alive, but it can be overcome.

"For instance, I am from the Somali community, but I disagree with female gender mutilation.

"Cultures are not static. They evolve and these practices have to be repudiated. But that won't happen while they are kept secret."

Zainab is based at the Newham Afro-Caribbean and Asian advocacy project (NACAAP) in Stratford Advice Arcade. She works within the Community Partnership Project between eight London boroughs.

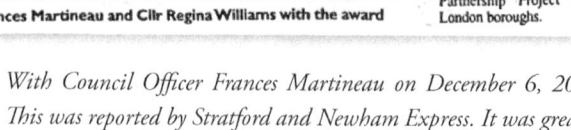

● **Frances Martineau and Cllr Regina Williams with the award**

With Council Officer Frances Martineau on December 6, 2006. This was reported by Stratford and Newham Express. It was great to be recognized for our efforts.

GREY skies and downpours did not deter about 150 people from taking a last look at the Olympic Park site. They joined athletes and councillors for the final walk of a series run by Newham council. More than 2,000 strollers have seen tranquil waterways, urban landscapes and historical buildings along the route. The site will now be closed to build facilities including the 80,000-seater Olympic stadium and Aquatics centre. Pictured are Cllr Regina Williams, Cllr David Griffin, Mayor of Newham Sir Robin Wales, Olympic gold medallists Tessa Sanderson and Daley Thompson and walkers at Three Mills.

Visiting the Olympic site - Our last glimpse before demolitions started for the construction of the 2012 London Olympics Stadium.

The Olympic Stadium in Stratford is now the home of the local West Ham United Football Club. I was a councillor for Stratford during the run-up to the London 2012 Olympics and sat on the committee that discussed the process of decanting local people from the site while catering for their interests.

Volunteering in the Community

As a community activist, I campaigned for better housing, school facilities for children, and childcare facilities to support single mothers in finding care for their young ones. Going to university in trains with my baby for three years motivated me to ensure other single parents in my area never went through this. I wanted them to have centers close to their homes where they could safely leave their kids and then go to university.

I volunteered to cover as a Catechism support teacher even when I was heavily pregnant in the year 2002.

CHAPTER FIFTEEN

DISCOVERING MY DATE OF BIRTH

I didn't know my actual date of birth because our family's record book, where my dad had recorded our birthdates, was either lost or destroyed. When I reached O Levels (equivalent to GCSE), I needed an ID card, and government officials were issuing them at my boarding school. Since I was consistently the oldest in my class and wanted to fit in, I chose the year 1965, like most of my classmates, and selected December 25, 1965, as my birthdate because it was Christmas Day and was easy to remember going forward. However, this was not my actual date of birth. I used it to obtain my ID because I didn't know my actual birthdate. I always appeared older than my classmates, which made me the target of bullying. So, I chose this date to fit in with everyone else in my class.

After many years of celebrating a guessed date of birth, I was fed up. My birthday never felt like an actual birthday. I knew that my parents baptised their children when they were young, maybe one month old, because they were staunch Catholics, and they would not dare let their baby grow up without baptism. They called it 'handing their baby to God.'

So, I decided that when I returned home, I would go to the church where my mum baptised her children to search the books. Because it was a big mission, I knew I would get the truth. I'd look for my baptism card, which would reveal when I was baptised and include the name of my godmother. My mother had told me who my godmother was, so I had that clue, too.

My dad used to keep a little brown book in his coat pocket—a very small book where he had written all our dates of birth. This book was always with him. I don't know what happened to the book. It may have gotten burned in the house or misplaced. Bless him—I miss him even more when I think about him always carrying his precious book.

The church was in the Parish of Nyabururu. Mum told me I was the last one in the family to be baptised there because a new church was built near home. When my sister Stella and my brother Ken came, they were baptised at the new church.

I called the parish and made an appointment. I would start with two dates: the birthdate of my late elder brother, the one I follow, and the birthdate of our late twin brothers. I knew I was born between those dates. With the help of a nun, I started searching the books from 1962 to 1965. We didn't go far; we found the truth among the records for the first year, 1962.

When I saw it, I screamed, 'Yes! Yes!' I was over the moon; the nun who was searching within the parish made me a baptism card that showed my date of birth. Immediately, I called my family in London to tell them the good news. The mystery was solved. I made several copies of that card and saved its image to my cloud to make sure it would never be lost again.

I thought about my dad and the little book. Dad never had iCloud—or even a computer, Google Drive or OneDrive. When I walked into the church, based on the date I'd been using as a birthday, I was 50. That day, I discovered I was 54 years old.

PART III:

DEALING WITH GRIEF

CHAPTER SIXTEEN
DEATHS IN THE FAMILY

Dad's death 4th May 1997

From the left at the back are Teresa, Philomena, and me. In the front from left are Alex, our father, and Lawrence. Lawrence was my parents' first grandchild and, therefore, always special. This picture means a lot to me because Dad and Alex have since departed, and it is the earliest of me and my dad. This was taken outside Teresa's house at Dr Kraft Memorial Secondary School Rabai, Mombasa.

Around 1978-1979 - from Left to Right: Alex, Teresa and my dad. Notice how Teresa is wearing platforms but the rest are in slippers. This was done deliberately to give her some height because she is the shortest in our family. Teresa was always dad's girl.

I had minimal interaction with my dad as a child. For much of my childhood, he lived away from our homestead. It's not that I did not know him. It's more that he was a distant figure, someone I knew was important but not present every day.

My plans after leaving Kenya were to complete my education, return home, get a job, assist my parents in educating my siblings, provide for my family's day-to-day needs, and spend time with my father. This was a significant ambition for me as a young woman; I wanted to get to know Dad. He always talked about a time when his children would flourish financially and set up family businesses to liberate the family from poverty. It was one of my longings to do so. Unfortunately, it took too long for me to get immigration papers in the UK, and as fate would have it, he passed away in 1997. I couldn't attend his funeral since doing so would lock me out of the UK. This was one of the most painful seasons of my life. I hadn't seen him for almost ten years. He never had a chance to witness and enjoy my success, and he never saw my children. This was absolutely heartbreaking for me. As a strong Christian, I hope to reunite with him in the life to come under the loving leadership of Jesus Christ. My father was a prayerful man and a staunch Roman Catholic. I believe that his spirit is in paradise, awaiting the resurrection of the saints. I share the faith, knowing one day, I'll be with him again.

Alex's death 1st April 2003

My brother Alex kept himself fit, in fact very fit. He worked out. He went on long morning or evening runs, sometimes both of us on the same day. Back from the run, Alex would eat a whole basket of oranges and mangoes, consumed with six eggs and a full flask of tea! We would complain about this, but we didn't appreciate how much his rigorous exercise, along

Alex and me. This picture was taken in1978.

We visited a studio in Kisii town to take this picture. I wore Alex's jacket for the snapshot. I was in slippers because I didn't have shoes. They were too expensive. This is likely the earliest picture of me, taken before I started secondary school. I don't have any pictures of myself as a toddler. For the photo shoot, Alex wore his bell-bottom trousers, which were hugely popular at the time, along with matching platform shoes. Alex's sense of fashion encouraged me to study hard and to dress as impressively as he did. Take note of Alex's afro hairstyle – my brother truly had a flair for fashion.

with the heat of Mombasa, sapped his energy and how much he had to eat to replenish himself. Honestly, we thought he was greedy. How wrong we were! And now, I exercise a bit and know what it means to eat well after swimming or a long walk. Thank God Mombasa is blessed with fruits.

Before he passed away in 2003, Alex and I discussed and agreed that I would visit him and his family in the US. I was looking forward to the trip, but Alex died before it could be arranged. His passing still pains me to this day. I guess the pain will reduce with time but will never go away completely. I always think about Alex and ask myself what the family would be like if he were still with us. Of course, I believe he would be doing wonderfully well for the family. He worked hard throughout his short life.

I long for the days we could have sat as adults and checked out our family vision, noting each other's struggles and achievements. Oh, the loneliness of missing my brother! I miss the adult talk and laughter we could have had, remembering our childhood, talking about our children, reminiscing about 'swimming' in the river, and killing birds for food, not knowing which bird was edible and which was not; thinking back to the absolute poverty that dominated the early years. We were playmates and were close. We shared many moments that pepper my memory with laughter against a background of fear and hunger.

He went without preparing any of us for it. He had chatted with Stella and Ken the previous day and was all fine, only to die the following day. We never saw it coming because he wasn't sick. He dropped off his kids at daycare and went to work. On returning from work, he felt sick, but there was nobody at home yet. He staggered to his tenants and knocked weakly on the door. He was calling his mother. They called 911, he was taken to the hospital, and he was put on life support. By 10 o'clock that evening, his wife had to make the tough decision to turn off the life support. Alex was gone. I cannot stop thinking about Alex, and I am yet to get over the pain that comes with that thought. My brother, Alex, was named Angwenyi after my dad's first brother, who passed away before my dad was born.

My brother was handsome, fun, and caring. I will keep him alive in this book. He was a sports enthusiast and practised boxing and karate while studying chemical engineering. When we were together in Mombasa, he encouraged me to join him for his morning runs. I would try, but he was fitter, faster and stamina-laden. He would quickly disappear on a long road in Kilifi County, and we would only reunite on his return. I have such memories!

Alex had a deep affection for children and found joy in taking his nieces and nephews out for walks. It is heartbreaking that he passed away at an early age, leaving a void in the lives of all in his family, particularly his wife, mother and two daughters in America, aged five and three at the time of his passing and two sons and a grandchild in Kenya. It's incredibly saddening when a father is taken away from his children at such a young age. In addition, he hadn't been able to see his children in Kenya since 1989, fourteen years before his passing on to everlasting joy. The pain of separation is one that only God can truly ease.

His premature death robbed me of the opportunity to share our life experiences as adults, enjoying our success while reflecting on our difficult backgrounds. This remains heartbreaking to me. I keep saying it could have been this or that if only he were around, and sometimes I feel that I do some of the stuff he could be taking care of.

There is much sorrow in life, particularly when a family member you were close to moves away to another country (as did I). Time passes, and everyday things get in the way of travelling to get together again. Then, quite suddenly, it's too late. We were talking about my going to America to see him and his family, and then he died. Like my father, I feel the ache inside me that we haven't been together for so long. There is much sorrow in life, but we also have our memories to sustain us.

Mum's death 13th September 2021

I cherish the memory of my mother's resilience during her decade-long battle with Alzheimer's and dementia. Her joyful spirit endured even as her health declined, particularly in the last two years. She struggled with memory loss, unable to recall her own children's names, yet music became a constant source of joy for her. During my visits, we were often dancing and enjoying music together.

Despite her fading memory, we maintained a special connection. From my home in London, we would share moments over the phone, singing and praying together, often Catholic songs because Mum was a staunch Catholic. These recorded conversations hold a special place in my heart, a testament to her unwavering spirit. However, during her last four months, as she wrestled with prayers and recitations, it became clear that her journey was nearing its end. Her condition deteriorated rapidly, and she had wounds, which tore my heart, but she found peace in her passing, surrounded by loved ones in Narok. The memories of our bond through music and faith will forever be with me and grace the pages of my autobiography.

Despite her early struggles with being a parent, my Mum was the family pillar, the cornerstone that I didn't fully appreciate until she was gone. Regardless of how old she was, I always knew I had a mother to look forward to when I returned to Kenya. The void left by her absence is one that nobody can fill. She held our family together; now, home will never be the same without her and Dad's presence.

I feel like a butterfly flying away alone. I sense the loss of my Mum has placed me in a world of freedom—not in a negative way, but for the first time, I have the liberty to move forward and do whatever I choose. Mum was the overseer of my actions, and it's as if I'm in a class without a classroom monitor.

Yet, I find solace in the fact that she has finally found comfort in the Lord, whom she loved so dearly.

Mum is the only person in the world to whom I could tell everything, whether good, bad, silly, or stupid, and never be afraid that she would tell or be ashamed of me anywhere. She's the only person I could have a heated discussion with and later have a great laugh with. She was the one who would tell me how mad I was over many things but also how good-hearted I was. As usual, she was right. I trusted her. Despite my mischief, the relationship with my mum was always warm, with true love as its base. You only get one mother in this world, so don't ignore all she is because once she exits the world, that is it, absolutely it, no matter how much you bite your lips when she's gone. Be with her, and do things with and for her. If I could rewind the clock, I would tell her how much I loved her, do her shoelaces, and then say goodbye, sweet Mum.

Mothers are extraordinary beings, no doubt about that, and I'd do anything to bring her back, even if only to shout at me as she often did; I would keep calm through her anger because I knew how much she loved me. On reflection, she was building me, and she did indeed make me in spirit, such that all her giving (and forgiving others for wrongdoing to cultivate peace) and helping for the sake of community and humanity came straight from her.

This book is about blessed struggles along the way of a journey. That journey is from one place to a better and different place. It can be a physical journey or a mental or emotional one. It can be all three different elements for other people.

Mum was on a journey. It wasn't remotely like mine, yet there were similarities. I've mentioned leadership—her in her old community and me in my new one. That's a definite parallel. But my journey had education at its core, and Mum remained illiterate all her life. Her journey started similarly to mine. We were both born into poor Kenyan families, although mine was more desperate than her origins. Then, her journey diverged. She wanted to become a nun, but her father said no; her value was in her dowry. She married Dad and found happiness of some sort. Yet her blessed struggle was being a parent. She had such great faith and spread her love around in true Christian fashion. I would have found it easier as a young girl if she had been able to say 'no' to strangers and concentrate instead on her family and children.

Then she turned to drinking due to depression, and mainly because of the drink, we were left to fend for ourselves. That made us grow up quickly—perhaps too quickly—missing out on being kids and teenagers.

Then Mum, Dad and all of us went stay at the mission (Catholic Parish of Ichuni), which was arranged by my sister, Teresa. This was her lowest point, and immense depression set in. Hence, she was often away, sometimes for weeks, leaving us with our sick dad on occasion. I believe she did this partly due to homesickness. She would visit her friends in our home in Nyakongo, the place we had left. Afterwards, she would continue her journey to her homeland, 'Bogeka', where she would visit her nephews and nieces whose parents had passed away. She felt a responsibility to care for them emotionally. Somehow, through all this, Mum found her way again. She rose from the dark nights of her despair and went out into the new day, discovering hidden talents for being a community leader and, eventually, becoming the pillar of her family once again.

Her journey may have taken her full circle, but it is, nonetheless, a journey. She found strength long after she lost it. She turned the weaknesses that had plagued her life into new strengths, always finding solace and fortitude in her faith.

Our Mum was a prayer warrior. May she rest in peace.

Mum and me. In 2000, I went back to the mission in Inchuni parish in Keroka, where we lived before I left Kenya; it was a day of reflection for both of us. The priest's house looked the same. I'm glad I went to reflect with my mum, looking back to those years of no freedom and deprivation for me as a young adult. It was not easy to live in a mission with little in terms of social life.

This time I was a councillor in London, and my Mum was a community leader in Nyakongo, our homeland.

MUMS FUNERAL 1ST OCTOBER 2021

On October 1st, 2021, we said our goodbyes to Mum as we stood at her grave together as siblings, feeling the weight of our loss yet holding onto each other for support.

In the front row from left to right are my sister Teresa, brother Ken, sister Philomena, sister Stella and me.

*1st October 2021-from left to right my sister Stella,
Kens wife Beatrice, Ken, me, Philomena, and Teresa*

William's death 13th December 2021

This news came as a complete shock in my life, leaving me with a profound sense of heartbreak, tears, and the harsh reality of death. "It was a significant loss - the premature death of a healthy man, just ten days shy of his 55th birthday, having recently retired from the Central Bank of Kenya. He hadn't established a proper bond with our son. It was truly sad. It was hard to take in. It put me in a lonely universe, my own invisible world of brokenness, surrounded by many yet alone often. I had God's comfort. I'm a very emotional person, something I didn't find out until the death of my Mum. Then, just three months after losing her, Willy died. Losing two of the closest people to me at an interval of only three months was a complete blow to my mind, like a balloon with all its air escaping at once. I was all alone in this second death, except for the saving grace and comforting presence of my young sister, Stella. Despite having met Willy only twice in Nairobi, she realised how warm the man was.

Six days before William's tragic passing, we had a conversation. I shared my intention to buy an apartment there in Mombasa, seeking his advice on the location. He suggested Nyali as the ideal choice. However, as I was preparing for my trip and checking in for my flight, I received a devastating call from his sister, Penina. She initially phoned me, informing me of a road accident involving three brothers, with William being seriously injured. I implored her to rush to his side, keep me updated on his condition, and told her that I was travelling to Kenya the following day. Just ten minutes later, she called me back, her voice filled with tears, and said, 'Regina, William died.' Our grief overwhelmed us, and we cried together over the phone, inconsolable.

The following day, upon my arrival in Kenya, I called his brother Alex, and he kindly offered to take me to the morgue to visit him the next day. I will forever appreciate Alex for his support. It was a heart-wrenching experience to witness Willy's lifeless body with closed eyes. Beside me stood his brother Alex next to me as I struggled to speak to him. He could not hear me. This stark reality pierced through me that once the eyes shut and the lips fall silent in death, words lose their power and meaning. Nonetheless, I'm grateful I had the opportunity to visit him in the morgue. It was there that I fully grasped his departure into the unknown realms of the afterlife.

This visit to the morgue was a moment I believe brought him solace in heaven.

Then, from the morgue, we drove to his parent's home, and on the way, I had the opportunity to see where the fatal accident took place. At home, I passed my deepest condolences to his family, who have known me as their own for years even though me and Willy went separate ways. We were there for an hour, and then we went back to pick up our flight to Mombasa. I did my best for Willy. I had never been to the morgue and found myself talking to the dead, but I did this, and I guess it is well in my soul. In 1999, we went our separate ways romantically and remained best friends, but now, separated by his death.

In my recollections during my time with Willy, he stands out as easygoing, a gentle giant with big dimples, kind, won't hurt anybody, no jealousy, and no competition with anybody. His presence remains vivid in my heart as part of my journey. I never thought I would be describing him when he is gone. Willy left this world so early.

In 1989, in the busy streets of Rabat, a photograph captured a memorable moment of Willy. We often strolled through the vibrant lanes of Avenue Mohammed V in Rabat capital of Morocco, recalling our shared adventures. Even after 35 years, the memory of Willy remains lively, carved in the corridors of my mind, unchanged from the days we roamed those streets together.

Keeping Memories and Love Alive: end of an era. R.I.P.

PART IV:

CONCLUSION

Your journey may not mirror mine exactly, but when you boil it down, like distilling spirits as we did back home, the essence remains the same. Ultimately, you are the owner of your life. You can make it better or worse, and I encourage you to try. Too many people resign themselves to a life of discontent, yet most of us have the potential to change our circumstances. My book is to show you what I did in the hope that you can apply the same effort and the same resilience and come out on top.

Just like I did.

My life has been challenging, and I'm not ashamed of telling it. I keep saying I never knew how beautiful I was because I had no time to look at myself in the mirror, to admire myself. I was overwhelmed by problems arising from an almost impossible background, a background of deprivation marked by the twin aspects of fear and hunger.

Fear and hunger can be crippling, building up to a point that will crush most people. Somehow, it did not crush me. I learned to fight back. I kept reminding myself that, as the proverb says, 'God helps those who help themselves.'

I helped myself to a better life. It took a lot of struggles, Blessed Struggles.

These were blessed struggles – tough, undoubtedly, but ultimately, I came out to the other side successfully.

Never give up, no matter what. Be persistent. Be like a cactus tree. The cactus tree survives in conditions of extreme drought, and in fact, it not only survives but often flourishes during long spells of drought and yes, I, too, have survived long spells of absolute darkness in my journey.

However difficult and bleak your circumstances look, keep moving no matter how slow the pace may seem, as long as the movement is forward.

In due time, all things will work together for your own good.

Look at me,

- Born and raised in abject poverty in rural Kenya.

- Took up adult/parental roles in childhood for my young siblings.

- Had my primary education interrupted for two years so I could take care of my sister's child.

- Severely bullied in school due to my age and in the community for crying during female circumcision.

- As a child, I used to craft traditional beer to sell, using the earnings to pay for my school fees, exercise books, pencils, and school. uniforms. Hardly had enough to eat as a child and young adult.

- Struggled with lack of food whilst learning a new language to study medicine in Casablanca.

- As if that was not enough hardship, I migrated to the United Kingdom pregnant with no money, no relatives or friends and, of course, massive culture shock.

Through all these obstacles/setbacks, God not only provided for my basic needs but also rewarded my effort with a university education, a great family, a splendid work experience across Europe and a 10-year political leadership in London- a world-class city. So, you too can make it no matter your gender, family background or country/continent that you are born into.

From my experience, I have only learnt that if you do your part and never give up, you will achieve whatever you want.

CHAPTER SEVENTEEN

MY DREAMS WERE
TO COME TRUE

You too can make it.

You have read about what I came through to be where I am today; they were struggles that have made me into who I now am.

Persistence pays off—be resilient like a cactus tree.

You can try and try until you find what you're looking for. If you try a path but meet a roadblock, you must make a U-turn and see where another road is. I'm simply saying: search in the North; if you can't find what you are looking for, then head South; if there is nothing in the South, turn East; and if there is nothing in the East, go West or from left, go to the right. Keep trying until you find it. As some will say, 'think out of the box'. In life, stagnation is not an option.

Sometimes, people who know I'm drafting this book ask me not to reveal too much, but if I do not, it won't truly represent my early life. I want people to see and understand that life can be difficult in some parts of this world, and when one is blessed in countries such as the UK, we should count our blessings and work hard to continue to change our lives and those of other people. The toughness of life energises me to press on and get the results I want for myself, my family, and others.

If someone prays and says, 'God, help me pass my exam,' but does not do any revision for that exam, then that person is doomed. It is not enough to ask God to help one pass an examination and then not prepare for one's tests. Passing an exam takes much more. Getting the right answers takes self-sacrifice, waking up early, preparation, hard work, determination, and long hours of revision.

What you do each day contributes to the final goal to turn your life around. When you have an opportunity to do something, for pity's sake, don't waste it because you will never see it again. Do not let any opportunity pass you by, like a blowing wind sends tumbleweed scuttling down the road and gone from your view. You can come out of any mess one day if you continue pushing forward. That is precisely what I have done, and I have, in turn, changed many people's lives.

God helps those who help themselves.

That's what makes my struggles blessed: the determination to succeed. It wasn't the way I thought I would make it. When in Morocco, I always imagined that I would return to Kenya, get a decent job, and help my family. Instead, I went down a different path altogether.

From my humble beginnings in Nyakongo, where we had a mud house with a thatched roof full of holes, frequent rains, seeing the moon and stars at night, no blankets and cold nights, encounters with safari ants and rats, in the house, eating my mother's heel and lacking basic amenities like a bed, tables, electricity, running water, and toilets – we used bushes for a bathroom and plant leaves as tissue. I slept on the floor with a group of girls, each pulling away whatever we had as covers or blankets: if you did not sleep in the middle you would be uncovered because each end person at the end pulls the blanket. Many days were marked by hunger, and affording school fees or even basic school supplies like pencils was a constant challenge. I often had to cut a single pencil into three for backup.

How many things do we take for granted nowadays? We have cakes, soft drinks, cereal, pocket money, sugar, salt, tea, rice, chicken, clothes, warm blankets and beds, and a kitchen fridge stocked with food. Each child has their own bedroom. We can boil water when we need it; just turn on a tap and flick a switch the list is endless, even including shoes and socks - I never had those when I was growing up.

One can appreciate hot water. Please thank God for all that we have. Imagine, like when I was in high school, that you arrive back from preps to find that someone has stolen the water from under your bed in your basin, and you have to beg friends for maybe two or three cups of water to wash with and then you start with your face and finish with your private parts. Can you imagine using just a couple of cups of water to clean yourself each morning before you go to assembly?

It sometimes felt like a surreal journey. The transformation and opportunities that have come my way have been beyond my wildest imagination.

And this is why I am grateful for living in Great Britain. I was able to access opportunities which I had dreamt of. I had somehow established in my mind and soul that there was no way I would fail in Great Britain. If I had managed to make it in the first year of medical school in Casablanca, learning French for the first time, and going on to do a degree and passing my first-year examinations at a tough time and with limited funds for my upkeep, I could not fail in the UK. I was hardened, and I had self-belief. I did not know a word of French when I set foot in Morocco, yet within a year, I was a good speaker of the language and even passed my first degree in medicine, taught in French. So, there was no way I could think I would not succeed in the UK, where everyone speaks and studies English.

Like many foreigners, it took me some time to accept that England is now my home. Initially, my goal was to pursue an education and return to Kenya as quickly as possible. However, that perspective changed when I realised that wherever one finds themselves, that place is home. Home is not defined by a location but by the people and connections you make. So, whoever is next to you becomes like a sister, brother, mother, father, and neighbour, no matter where you are in the world. England didn't define me, but it provided the environment, and I worked diligently despite the challenges, especially during the earlier years.

You can imagine, therefore, how I embraced my new life in the UK. I felt that it was an opportunity for me to change my story. I was excited that I had a council house. It had running water. I had some money for food, and I had electricity. For me, this was more than I needed.

I consider my struggles a blessing. I've been pushing myself for more. When my son was young, I realised I had to make a difference. I made excuses a few times in the UK, then accepted that the world is moving, and nobody waits for somebody else. I was asking myself questions:

Who cares that I am a single parent?
Who will care for you or love you if not yourself?
Who will sacrifice anything for you?

My answer to all these questions was that it was up to me to improve my situation. Study harder and longer to achieve better grades, then work harder and longer for better wages and investment.

I pulled through under very strenuous conditions. You can make it even without a family or relatives, entirely on your own if needed.

I remember when I first came to this country. I'll never forget seeing on the news that black and minority ethnic people in London were dying earlier from depression. Then I turned and looked at my sister on the settee in our council flat and asked her: why are they depressed? Isn't it better here than in many other places?

Then I told my sister: We have a home, running water, hot water to bathe in, and money for food—I couldn't think of what else we could want. We had come from nothing to comfort, and we were counting our blessings.

Later in life, I realised why depression was on the news. It's crucial to recognise that there are certain challenges that exist in society that hold others back, but we must rise above them. Otherwise, we will continue to struggle from one generation to the next. Sometimes, there is some form of discrimination in job recruitment, housing, hospitals, and education—for example, single parents, immigrants, and ethnic minorities. Let's strive to break down those barriers, believing that all people are equal and can indeed succeed.

History repeats itself when others are unwilling to stretch and change it.

Some take history from their parents' example, taking a casual attitude that they are poor and can never rise. NO. Press on and ARISE. Take any opportunity. Start small, and do not sit back, complaining and blaming others for your failure. Just do what you can, and do not create excuses for your failure. Do not take anything for granted. There are people who cannot afford a single thing, but they keep pushing hard for success.

For me, the biggest assistance I received in England was when I needed to provide milk for my child. Living among African students who relied on pocket money from their parents in Africa, made it challenging to put food on the table. I'll never forget diluting Kiora black currant drink to stimulate milk production. Though it wasn't the most balanced diet, it brought relief to see milk coming from my breasts.

Reflecting on those moments, I consider it a blessing that England provided assistance through Milk Tokens, for SM Gold Milk from the DSS. It was a lifeline for my child's well-being. Despite the challenges, I'm forever grateful for the support England provided, making it the ideal place for my child to begin his life.

In England, there was no discrimination in providing milk to newborns, every child born had access to milk, a fact I wasn't aware of at the time.

When you come from a background of hardship and scarcity, you get easily appeased by whatever you get. However, I soon found that I could not settle for less when more extraordinary things were achievable.

Our capabilities are limitless; the only boundary is the sky, and if we can find a way to soar through it, the possibilities are endless.

As the Bible teaches, the presence of God enables one to tread upon serpents without harm, and to rest with lions as Daniel did, emerging unscathed. Just as God sent an angel to protect Daniel, ensuring his survival, I am also a living testament to His watchful care and you too can be alive, tread on.

'Daniel's Answer to the King' (1892) by Briton Riviere. In this picture, you can see Daniel is focused on higher, even facing up. He is not focused on the lions behind him. So, in life, we must not focus on the difficulties around us. Because there is a sunny day, it will not always be difficult. So, as Daniel gazed ahead, he finally was taken out of this den of lions alive, not touched. And so, shall you succeed in your journeys, and your hardship will not consume you.

So, don't give up. You, too, will survive and reach the destination you want. When you get there, stretch out your hand and help somebody to change their life, too. It's also about changing the world around us, making it better for humanity.

There is too much noise, and people sometimes can't even hear their inner call. Make sure you can hear God's calling and walk the path that God wants you to tread. We all have to try and do what we can in the circumstances we find ourselves in.

During the most challenging time of my life, when I was a single parent, an immigrant black woman, and had no family to rely on, I somehow learned the importance of being kind and helping others. It's still a bit surprising to me. I remember how I used to buy second-hand clothes for my son and me, even though we could have bought new ones, to save money for our future and to help others.

The Abbey National Instant Saver book included here shows how I saved up £4,000 over a long time and finally withdrew £3,000, of which I sent £2,000 to William for his ticket. I wanted him to come here to help me raise our son. I sent the other £1,000 to my family in Kenya. Looking through my savings book, I realise there are times when I went to the post office to deposit just £5, and there are times when I could withdraw £10 or £5. And when I withdrew this money, I used it to buy carrots, potatoes, milk, sugar and bread, the essentials for my kitchen, and I would save the rest. I was frugal, so there were no strawberries, blueberries, or other stuff I found expensive. Of course, I didn't buy fast food. The week I didn't need to buy nappies for my son was when I saved the most from my benefits. How I did this is beyond my thinking. My income support at that time was £56 a week. It's incredible how I could make it last and save a little here and there.

Sometimes, I was lonely, but the baby kept me busy, and my faith in God did the impossible. Take it from me: I was better off than I was growing up in my country of birth and in Morocco, where I started my university education.

RECEIPTS £ p	WITHDRAWALS £ p	BALANCE £ p
		3195.7
	10.00	3185.70
		3195.70
10.00		
	10.00	3185.70
	10.00	3175.70
	40.00	3135.70
	5.00	3130.70
120.00		3250.70
180.00		3430.70
10.00		3440.70
	5.00	3435.70
	10.00	3425.70
		3435.70
	10.00	3425.70
	5.00	3420.70
200.95		3621.65
	5.00	3616.65
150.00		3766.65
310.00		4076.65
	10.00	4066.65
10.00		4076.65
	20.00	4056.65
80.00		4136.65
	3015.00	1121.65
		1121.65
5.00		1126.65
84.36		1211.01
	10.00	1201.01
	40.00	1161.01
10.00		1171.01

My first significant saving and first massive withdrawal of savings to help others, a pivotal moment in my life—a moment not just for personal gain, but as a steppingstone to extend a helping hand to others.

I remember a conversation I had with my son when he was older. I showed him the transaction I made to try bringing his dad to Britain so that we could be a family, together and happy. My son had never known about this before. I told him that it was done in 1993 when he was only two-and-a-half years old. By then, William was already settled in a responsible job at the Central Bank of Kenya and, was not keen to come to the UK. I didn't want to lose my papers by leaving the country and wanted our son to be in the UK, where we both reckoned, he had opportunities galore.

Willy waited nine years for the two of us to join him, but unfortunately, obtaining citizenship took longer than anticipated. In the end, it seems that life took us on separate paths. Life is a complex puzzle, and sometimes, we cannot piece it all together. Only with hindsight can we see how it was meant to be.

There is a link from one friendship to another. For example, my friend Obutu and I stood together through fear and terror. We helped each other because of that friendship. She helped me, and now I can help her son.

I knew that Obutu had a son, and I longed to establish contact with him and tell him how wonderful his mother had been. In his mother's family, his uncles and grandparents had passed away, so this child had nobody to support him; the mother, Obutu, had never married, and the son didn't know his father. It took years before we finally reconnected. I met the boy in 2000 when he was only six or seven years old and promised to look after him. But on returning to the UK, all inquiries I made were fruitless because nobody would tell me where the boy was. But the boy himself eventually caught up with me through Facebook. Thank God for Facebook. He came across my sister Stella's page in 2020. Since then, we have been in touch, and I have supported him financially and helped him fulfil his dream of being a driver.

I put my trust in God, knowing that he watches over me. Yet, unlike my mother and father, I also put my trust in myself, digging deep into my reserves of resilience. I knew, instinctively perhaps, that God helps those who help themselves.

With no support systems for my parents, they left all worries to God to take over. That was very much my mother's motto, and somehow, it worked for her because we are all successful, and I believe God took over for them. Instead of placing blame on my parents, I endeavoured to work diligently in order to alleviate the deprivation they experienced in life.

They still had their faith, enormous faith in God. Mum spread her immense love too thinly, like butter barely touching the bread, to everyone in her community. It was a case of caring for too many people, trying to love them all equally, to the point that we, her children, felt that our portion of that love was reduced because it was given so widely.

I don't think that way. I have a stark contrast with my parents when it comes to dealing with hardships. I had to fight my childhood hardships, and as a foreign, a single parent, and a member of a minority group with no family, I faced various forms of discrimination. However, I had to overcome these challenges, stand tall, and strive not just for survival but to truly live and succeed in life. There was no way out but to face situations as they came. Yes, I ask God to help me every day through prayer. But I have learned two things. First, God helps those who help themselves. Second, hard work produces results and realities in life must be faced and not shy away from it.

God has given us immense and unlimited capacity to achieve our dreams if we can do our part.

CHAPTER EIGHTEEN
TESTIMONIES

It is the state of want that causes people like me to run with every opportunity. The conditions in the UK are different from those in other countries. As a result, some people may not realise they have opportunities and, therefore, need to be supported by sharing inspiring stories like mine. I have seen the impact of sharing when one or two people have taken up the challenge and changed their lives. However, in places like the UK, most people have not seen the dark side of life, which is common in the developing world. There are no benefits in those parts of the world.

I have helped people just by talking to them, encouraging them, and giving them hope. One young woman I met had set her sights on getting a supermarket or cleaning job and settling down with it. I had a long talk with her and, would you believe it? She ended up going to university and graduating with a first-class honours degree. Now, she heads the MRI and Radiology Department in a private hospital and is the proud owner of a nice two-seater convertible car.

She bought a beautiful house for her family, a turning point in Kate's life. Kate has sent in testimony that I will include here as a motivation to others to make their lives successful and comfortable through the effort of hard work and study. Her endorsement makes me feel great. Kate invited me to her home to sit in the hot tub and relax. It was beautiful. I hadn't been in a hot tub before.

Kate represents one of my best success stories and one that I'm immensely proud of. I admire Kate because she lights up my world; she is testimony to the fact that one can move what appears unmovable if one puts one's mind to it. Kate's story will motivate you. This is a girl who was looking for a supermarket or cleaning job until I inspired her, and bang, she went from success to success. I have met people who encouraged me to write a book about my experiences, from growing up in my poor rural Kenyan village to becoming a people's elected representative in one of the world's most important metropolises. A colleague I worked with at the Ministry of Justice in London had an idea. She thought I would help pupils and students in the UK if I went to schools and colleges and gave talks and lectures about taking on challenges and succeeding in the missions one set for oneself.

My son once said, 'Mum, go ahead and write your book. Mum, you motivate me. I don't need to look anywhere for motivation, considering what you and Dad went through in North Africa.' My son didn't know that in Kenya, where I was born, there were significantly darker challenges than in Morocco.

At times, I had to look after my mother and father when they drank. I remember having sleepless nights when they threw up and then cleaning their smelly clothing the following day. This meant nights of fear that they might die, especially as this was in our village with no electricity or security or any emergency services; this haunts me to this day.

Yes, I had my parents, but sometimes it was like they were not there when it came to parental duties and even shifted these responsibilities to their children, meaning I was never a child. From the moment I started to understand the hell around me, I was looking after my siblings, with parental duties falling to me. It made me like an orphan, not entirely alone because of my siblings, but we, the children, often seemed to be the parents of the family.

You can imagine, therefore, that I readily embraced my new life in the UK. I saw it as an opportunity for me to change my story. I was excited that I had a council house. It had running water; I had some money for food, and we had electricity. For me, this was more than I needed. When you come from a background of hardship and scarcity, you get easily appeased by whatever you get. But I soon found out that I could not settle for less.

I have since been pushing myself for more. I was asking myself questions: I am a single parent. Who will care for me if I don't care for myself? Who loves me if I don't love myself? Who will sacrifice for me if I don't sacrifice for myself? Who will study harder and longer for myself if not me? I found out that the answer to all was me.

Testimony from Kate Davies, UK

One conversation with Regina completely changed my life. My perspective, my outlook on life, just... everything. I will never forget the day that a spark ignited in me and how she completely changed my life.

I give all credit to her.

And I know people might look at where I am in my life and think that I got myself there.

"But you got yourself where you are and single handedly put in the work, right?"

Wrong.

...Mostly.

Regina gave me the one crucial step - courage.

Courage helps you get out of bed to face the day.

Courage motivates you to hand in your dissertation that you've been going over and over to get right.

Courage lifts you up to give as many hugs as you can.

The courage to be unapologetically you.

In essence, without her, I couldn't be the strong, confident, and successful person I am today.

But it started with a stay-at-home mum who took a part-time job as a carer for the elderly. As much as I enjoyed my job, it wasn't sustainable after my second divorce, and I needed to pay my mortgage and bills somehow!

I've always been reasonably social and not particularly academic, so the idea of working in a supermarket has always appealed to me.

The excitement of getting an interview for a local supermarket was promptly shattered by rejection. So much was resting on getting a job there and it felt like my options were running thin.

Devastated, I called Regina, and was a little surprised at her reaction. She asked me why I was trying to get a job instead of going to university.

University?

At 31?

With four- and six-year-old children?

I couldn't even comprehend doing anything so...intense with my average GCSE grades.

Yet, that didn't deter Regina from encouraging me. I knew that Regina came from humble beginnings, and I had seen for myself the unbelievable achievement that spurred on my determination and spirit.

Now I just needed to work out what I wanted to study. Since I had my carer background, I thought it was best to build from that. I still wasn't taking myself very seriously in my mind, but I humoured myself with the choice.

I contacted the NHS careers helpline to discuss possible careers such as physiotherapist, occupational therapist, and radiographer.

At the mention of radiographer, I immediately wanted to know more - since I had no idea what it was. The more we chatted about it, the more I was interested.

All I could think about was Regina cheering me on, motivating me, giving me the courage to better myself.

In order to get my degree, I needed to attend college for Chemistry, physics, and biology. Going to college is hard enough without two small dependents, but I moved through; now, I am able to apply for my degree.

450 candidates.

To 55 places.

The odds weren't exactly in my favour, but I couldn't stop now, I'd got so far. I worked as hard as I could at the interview and was successful in getting a place. My euphoria was short lived as my first essay earned me 33%. Essay after essay, I tried harder and harder. Year one passed, year 2 passed. Then to my dissertation.

There are so many choices: a literature review, a clinical audit, or a research project. The latter was not recommended due to the difficulty of gaining ethical approval.

Of course, I had to choose it—it was the only one in my year, in fact (I think).

Once again, I beat the odds.

A first-class honours degree.

Me. A first-class honours degree in a science-based physics heavy subject.

That was 13 years ago now, and to this day, I still cannot believe this is my life; this is what I have achieved.

I had this potential all along, all my life. But it seemed only Regina saw it in me. Or at least enough to make me believe it myself.

I went from student to radiographer, to MRI radiographer, to senior radiographer, to lead MRI radiographer, and finally, where I am now, to deputy radiology manager. Every single time that I speak to Regina on the phone or in person, I thank her and credit her with everything I have today.

She admires my car - I say that it's because of you.

She admires my house - I say that it's because of you.

She comes to visit me at work - I say that it's because of you.

I still find it hard to comprehend that the power that was instilled in me that day has only just grown exponentially. I take any opportunity to tell the story because I want to share and promote the power that we all have within us, which sometimes needs another person to show us how to unlock.

I forever love and admire Regina for the wonderful person she is, for the inspirational person she is, my role model.

Testimony from Pamela, Kenya

A friend is someone who understands your past, believes in your future and accepts you just the way you are, and Regina is that friend to me. The universe has a strange way of connecting humans. There are people that come your way, and you don't hit it off instantaneously, and that was my encounter with Regina. When she joined my school in fifth grade, she was intimidating to me. She was very focused on her studies, while I liked to joke around and play pranks. She seemed to have clear goals and knew that hard work was necessary to achieve them. Meanwhile, I was more interested in having fun, making noise, and didn't mind the punishments I got at the end of every school day.

Regina quickly got used to her new surroundings. Kisii Primary was the top school in the county, and Regina stood out for being genuine and full of energy. These traits made her popular with the school's leaders, and she soon became the head girl, even though she had been there for less than a month. I often found myself in trouble and in her list for making noise, which meant I usually had to pick up trash in the schoolyard before going home. I thought she didn't like me, but years later, when we both ended up studying in the UK, I came to appreciate her strictness and understood that jokes do not fit well with academic success.

On completing our primary education, Regina passed very well and was called to Nyanchwa Secondary and later transferred to a prestigious Nyabururu Girls High School while I was called to Iterio mixed, a place I did not take up. We lost contact, and after high school University of Nairobi and learnt that Regina was on a scholarship to Morocco. Later, we reconnected in London. I was undertaking postgraduate studies, and she had just moved there and was pursuing studies on artificial intelligence - this sounded so crazy and alien to me. Back in the 90s, very little was known about this subject; she was ahead of the pack.

My encounter with Regina in the UK was different. I was now a professional, not the noise maker she knew. She was a mother to a lovely young boy, Emmanuel, and an aspiring artificial intelligence expert. We spent weekends babysitting Emmanuel, reminiscing about our childhood, and catching up with old primary schoolmates. Those were beautiful times. We became close and each other's keeper. On completion of my studies, I returned to Kenya while she stayed on in the UK.

As a councillor in Newham, Regina demonstrated what I had known all the time: the born leader that she was. For the young village girl from Nyankongo, a village no one thought much about, to be elected as a councillor in the United Kingdom for three terms was a big deal. I remember the pride with which I shared her number with all my friends who visited the UK, she was a truly inspiring, beautiful and generous soul who opened her home to all my friends who visited.

As Regina documents her journey from Nyankongo to Mukumu, then Morocco and the UK. I am elated and happy that our paths crossed again in our adulthood. Her strictness, though I didn't appreciate it as a noisy young girl, served me well later in life. A journey well-travelled and a good read for young people, an inspirational journey. You can be absolutely what you desire, and our destinies are in our own hands. We have the power to choose to succeed or to fail, and Regina is a true testimony to that. Regina, you are my hero.

CHAPTER NINETEEN
IN CONCLUSION

My life has not always been like this. My life was tough. My life was hard. I never imagined I would get to where I am now. As I've drafted this book, I've realised there are so many reasons for putting my story down on paper. These often intermingle as motives, forming a desire to see in print the struggles I've gone through; in total, they become me and my life story, whereas individually, they are the strands to my existence, aspirations I have to make it different for others.

I'm writing my story so my family can learn from my life experiences. I want my book to be a record of the blessed struggles I've undergone so that my children and those closest to me can see my travels in life, witness my journey and know the origin and the destination. Every journey is different; a mother's struggles are different from her child's. Yet, in many ways, the parent's destination is the child's starting point; I'm writing this so my children can see where I came from, my origins, and my struggles. I'm not sure I have told the entire story or scratched the surface. I hope it will form the basis for my children to appreciate their roots. I hope they will understand what I went through to be where I am. The foundation has been laid for them not to go through what I went through when growing up, but also hope they will go further, travel more than I've travelled, and push themselves further.

I hope that by sharing my story, someone - both those I know and those I will never meet - will be inspired to walk the journey of life, wherever it takes them, wherever they end up. Life is a journey for all of us. Whatever your faith (or lack of it), you must know that we humans are different; something within us makes us stand outside nature and means every life is an individual journey. Your responsibility is to put one foot in front of the other until you arrive.

I hope that by sharing my struggles, someone will be blessed by understanding that it does not matter where you came from. That it does not matter how many times you fall. And that if you do fall, fall forward. That all of us have a part to play to get where we want to be. The blame game does not help. Hard work pays off. Faith and hope are great ingredients for all. Life can be hard and full of mountains to climb. But you are a winner when you can climb that mountain and you are a winner when you get out of that valley, out of that tunnel of miseries, and move to happiness. Then success is when you have not given up and continue to battle with life to get to where you want to be.

I was, and still am, a fighter and a winner. You too can be a fighter and a winner because God is no respecter of persons (ACTS 10: 34-35).

I am grateful to God for the darkness I have already experienced, as it has led me to the light that I currently embrace. I also recognise that transforming and overcoming obstacles in life is key to shaping the world and bringing about positive change for all. My success has blessed many in my family, friends and strangers, both here in the UK and in Kenya. My original mission, was for me to get money and support my family, but now I have extended my mission to be about changing people's lives, either in small or big ways.

My life must touch others in order to call it successful, and that is what I am doing physically and emotionally by encouraging people through my motivational speaking. From night to day, from darkness to light, cold to warmth, fear to security and hunger to plenty. This has been my journey. It has not been easy, and there's no point in pretending. Life is full of struggles, and it is about overcoming them each day. Even deciding to be happy as you wake up each day is a struggle because you wake up and find issues waiting for you to resolve. We must rise above the problems blocking our happiness. A better destination is worth the struggle. Too many people settle back into a sad life, yet most of us can do something about it. You are the owner of your life; you can make it better or worse. There is nothing to lose. Don't die without reaching for your dreams.

I have shared my life journey to show what I have had to conquer and not to seek sympathy. I am hoping that readers will be encouraged to change and stretch things around them, knowing that hard work pays off. I have come a long way, and I believe that what you plant is what you harvest. At times, people want to achieve or see results very quickly, but sometimes, things take longer to be realised, so patience is key. Results don't come overnight. I have scaled hills and mountains from the valley of poverty.

Every individual can make a difference. I received help in wonderful ways. Each journey is different and stands alone, yet we can give and take help, and all our life stories are connected and intermingled in wonderful ways. Teresa gave me so much through her generosity of spirit, and I, in turn, have helped others; maybe it's a shallow reflection of the help I've received, but it's been given wholeheartedly and without reserve or condition.

Give and It Shall Be Given unto You

Luke 6:38 goes on to say:

For What Measure You Mete
It Shall Be Measured to You Again

I just want to thank God for helping me to tell it all. There is no point holding back some of my life experiences because this is the real me. Mine has been a story of hardship. A story of want. A story of struggle.

When I was hungry, I remembered verses in the Bible like Matthew 4:4, which says that 'man shall not live on bread alone but by every word that proceeds from the mouth.' This verse gave me strength to gaze ahead, and this was comforting and reassuring because I believed the hand of God was around my waist and hunger was not to claim my life. With two more verses below, I was armed to soldier on; Corinthians 10:13 and Isaiah 41 'No temptation has overtaken you' and 'Fear not, for I am with you.' I now had strength, solace, and a sense of purpose to continue the good fight, and it worked for me, and it will work for you, too. I hope the pages of Blessed Struggles have inspired and motivated you to face your fight in your journey.

I hope my story can make a difference in other people's lives and motivate them to fight to escape situations of want and deprivation. If I can do it, you most certainly can. Buckle up for the long haul; you will, one day, get there.

The most important things for me were focus, dreaming, and ensuring that that terrible history will not repeat itself. You know, people say history repeats itself - but hang on — even if that were the case, we must see which history we want to repeat itself. We must know our history. We must know where we are coming from to know where we are going. But we must put the bad history behind us. We must never repeat the bad history. We must keep a good history. I dreamt of changing the bad history. And this is me now.

I had to be focused and make sure that I would never sleep on the floor again and I would never sleep cold and hungry. I will never live a life of not knowing if I will have something to eat or have no period pads.

How many people appreciate switching on the kettle for tea and having a cup of tea within seconds? Very few people will appreciate it or even think about it. Unless you have been in a situation where there's no milk, no sugar, no firewood and not even water to enable you to have a cup of tea, you may not appreciate what you are taking for granted. Think for a moment what it means to lack every ingredient for a simple cup of tea, not just going without milk or sugar but without the fuel to heat the water, without even the water, for which you have to go to the pipe in the stream and wait your turn, accepting the bullying and ridicule from cruel people who have not even set out on their journey but prefer to make life miserable for those that have.

Forget the whole process of making a fire. Smoke goes into your eyes, especially if the firewood is not dry; there will be considerable smoke. The eyes go red; the fire does not burn continuously. It's on and off. So, for my precious cup of tea, we would have to kneel and blow into the fire to bring it on if it had burned out. I would push the wood into the fireplace and start blowing onto it, great big lungfuls, like we do to blow up a balloon, just to make the fire start burning. So full of smoke, tears rolling down my cheeks and nose running, but no tissues or handkerchief available, and all this just to make a cup of tea. Sometimes, if the embers in the fireplace had gone off, and I did not have a matchbox, I had to fetch fire from a neighbour's house. I could be given a few live pieces of charcoal in a tin to help light the fire in our house. I needed to have dry, thin firewood to light the fire. Also, many times, we pinched a bit of grass from the roof, as the house was grass-thatched, to start the fire.

Now, all I do is press the switch in the wall to turn on the lights, find the kettle, fill it from the kitchen tap, and plug it in to heat the water. Then I turn to the cupboard and pull out a teabag and the sugar pot, some milk from the fridge, and the cup, perhaps straight from the dishwasher. I can do this whenever I want.

Back home, you would be seriously scolded if you made tea for yourself after having had tea with the family in the morning because you would be wasting sugar meant for the following day's breakfast. Many times, Mum would hide sugar after morning tea so that nobody could find it and treat themselves.

At the age of 30, I was living in other people's houses. I had no money, nothing. It was difficult to have a cup of tea in other people's houses. The people loved me, but I was not comfortable making tea or eating what I wanted to eat, especially when I was pregnant, and I had a good appetite but no food. I remember I had a craving for pears and monkey nuts, but it was difficult to get them. And when my son was born, I had to stop breastfeeding because I had no food to eat to keep my breasts supplied. I had no benefits initially, so it was tough for my son. He did not have his SMA gold milk that almost every baby in Great Britain had because I did not know of his entitlement.

I could have perished. I never had food in the fridge and freezer as I do now, but I kept trying to create what I have today for myself, my family, and for the others that I have touched in some way, and I cherish my success in touching others.

I came here with my son in my tummy, but now I have a family of fourteen people. I call it my success.

I am sharing my story because I believe that someone will be impacted. I am sharing it with humility because I wasn't always like this.

Here are some lessons from the story of my life:

- Take risks, and do not be afraid of opportunities.
- Try, try, and try again. Don't give up. Even when you do give up, tell yourself in the morning that now you will try again.

The risk is to try. Taking a chance or attempting something new involves a degree of uncertainty or potential failure. However, it also suggests that the real risk lies in not making an attempt at all. By not trying, you might miss out on valuable opportunities, experiences, or knowledge that could enrich your life or lead to success. Embrace the uncertainty and challenges that come with trying new things. The greater risk lies in not taking any risks at all.

- You never know until you try.
- No good thing is easily found.

- Stay focused on the goals you have set for yourself.

- Do your part, play your part. Nobody will do it for you.

- If you are a leader or a mentor, then help others chart their course.

- Remain resilient like the cactus tree.

This is my message to young people and everybody needing advice. You may have a good education, but you do not have a good job. Do not give up. Fight on. Do not pick and choose when you have nothing substantial. Take what comes up and bide your time amidst hard work. Do not look to others to lift you up. They may disappoint you. Life has never been straight; things happen, and we feel down and lonely sometimes or very lonely, so don't start saying, 'I am breaking down; I can't go on.'

We can view life as a book with varied chapters. Trying new things is akin to turning the pages of a book - some chapters might be challenging, yet they contribute to our growth and learning experiences. Taking risks and trying new paths often lead to discovering valuable knowledge and finding joy in unexpected places. Embracing these opportunities, even if some are not as favourable, allows us to explore the vast richness that life has to offer.

As a Christian, the Bible says God will never give you more than you can take because, like a father or parent, you don't burden your kids too much but just enough to give them experience in life. From my experiences in life, when it looks so dark and seems almost impossible to believe, whether you will make it, believe me, and hold on because the light is not far from you. The darkest hour is just before dawn.

I thank God for my struggles. They have made me strong inside and able to take the storms in life. My struggles revealed the real me, resilient like the cactus tree, and gave me more faith in God.

They have turned out to be Blessed Struggles.

FAMILY PHOTOS

It's a beautiful picture capturing a moment during our visit to Kenya around 2016. In the photo, I am bending next to my younger brother Ken, while our mother sits nearby. My big sister Teresa stands tall, and my younger sister Stella bending to the left. It's a special memory of a family gathering during our visit to see our beloved mother in Kenya.

Another cherished memory from my visit to Kenya in 2017 to see my sick mum alongside my two beloved big sisters, Philomena on the left and Teresa on the right. Visiting my mum created an unforgettable and timeless moment that will forever be cherished and remembered among us.

My legacy, as I've shared, extends beyond material wealth—it's about the relationships forged, the tales recounted, and the memories safeguarded for my family. By compiling my family history and personal journey into a book, I aim to ensure that these narratives and images endure across generations, becoming treasured elements of our family heritage. My focus on memories, connections, and the impact on others reflects, I trust, a profound understanding of life's true significance. This legacy, grounded in love, shared experiences, and the human bonds I've cultivated, holds great worth and, I believe, will persist in the hearts and minds of those I've touched.

THE LIVING CACTUS TREE IS A SIGN OF
RESILIENCE TO TOUGH CONDITIONS –

I HAVE BEEN THERE.

I took this picture during my 2023 visit to the Masca Valley in Tenerife. I found further inspiration in discovering beautiful routes in the valley. This may look simple to others but I see how valley is full of challenges but the cactus trees thrive there. I witnessed beauty and growth, realizing that in life, like in this valley, there are opportunities to emerge onto a beautiful route from even the deepest challenges. This perspective reminds us to remain resilient and optimistic, knowing that there is always a way, a path leading to something better.

with all my love Regina Williams

Printed in Great Britain
by Amazon

41670934R00155